The Illustrated History of

SUNBEAM
Bicycles and Motorcycles

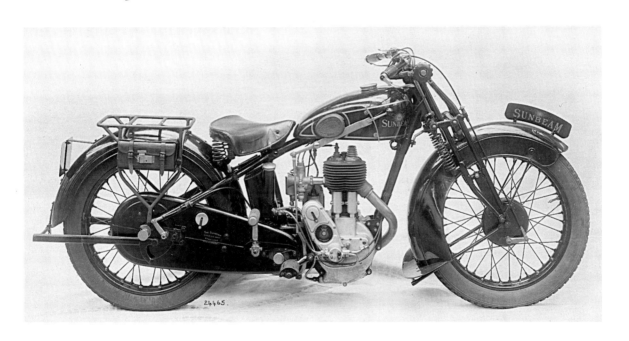

Robert Cordon Champ

Foulis

Haynes

Dedication

Dedicated to the memory of Bob Currie, whose careful interest, in the last months of his life, contributed much to this book.

ISBN 0 85429 688 3

© **Robert C. Champ 1989**

First published February 1989, reprinted November 1989

A FOULIS Motorcycling Book

Published by:
Haynes Publishing Group
Sparkford, Nr. Yeovil, Somerset BA22 7JJ, England

Haynes Publications Inc
861 Lawrence Drive, Newbury Park, California 91320 USA

British Library Cataloguing in Publication Data
Champ, Robert Cordon
The illustrated history of Sunbeam bicycles
and motorcycles. (General motorcycling).
1. Sunbeam bicycles, to 1987.   2. Sunbeam motorcycles, to 1987
I. Title.   II. Series.
629.2'272
ISBN 0-85429-688-3

Library of Congress Catalog Card No: 88-82504

Editor: Jeff Clew
Cover design: Phil Lyons
Layout design: Tim Rose

Printed in England by J.H. Haynes & Co. Ltd.

Introduction - 'The Sunbeam'

Established, said the catalogues, in 1790, though able to claim origins fifty years before that, the company which made 'The Sunbeam' is now one of the oldest in British industry. The firm's history was based amongst the tinplate manufacturers of Wolverhampton and its outer districts, where firms later adopted the Victorian fashion for japanned, or black-enamelled, ware, popular in imitation of the oriental originals.

John Marston was born in 1836, at Ludlow in Shropshire, and was apprenticed in 1851 to the Wolverhampton japanner Edward Perry, following a spell at a local iron works. After his apprenticeship, Marston purchased a nearby business and, when Perry died, in 1871, he amalgamated this with Richard Perry, Son & Co., thus becoming a major japanware manufacturer.

In 1887, 'Mr. John', as he was called in the Black-country fashion, decided to enter the up and coming bicycle trade, registering the trademark of 'Sunbeam' in January 1888. Three possible sources of the name: a suggestion by Ellen Marston, his wife, of 'Sunray', which name turning out to be already in use was then modified to Sunbeam; the use of part of verse two of Hymns Ancient and Modern No. 92 'Sunbeams scorching all the day', 'scorching' being a then current word for cycling fast; or Sunbeam from the sailing yacht of Lord and Lady Brassey, famous in Victorian times for its round the world voyage. (This was chronicled in 1878 by Lady Brassey under the title of 'A Voyage in the Sunbeam', later modified into an advertising slogan by John Marston.) The yacht was black, with a gold line, as was the Sunbeam cycle, but, then, much japanware was black with gold lines.

The truth, no doubt, lies in a combination of these ideas. By 1888, Marston was in business as 'John Marston, Paul St. Works, Wolverhampton, Tinplate Worker and Japanner, and Bicycle and Tricycle manufacturer.'

The new line was slow to move, but business improved after 1889 when the cycles were exhibited at that year's Stanley Show. The opening of a London showroom that May and expansion of staff numbers showed that Marston was serious about cycles and their production. The early machines were not of particularly noteworthy design though they were as well finished as might be expected of a leading japanware maker. The first catalogues show varied styles and it was not until 1892 that the watershed was reached. This was the adoption of Harrison Carter's chaincase, an ideal 'extra' for a tinplate manufacturer to use on a cycle. Soon christened the 'Little Oil Bath', the chaincase was to become a feature of Sunbeam cycles and motor cycles for seventy years.

Marston's policy became that of marketing a restricted range of designs and of trying to make them perfect, and in that he succeeded very well. At first, the prestige model in the cycle ranges was the 'Royal' (given the maker's code of V.R., though without any obvious regal patronage). In the 1900s this became the second model to the 'Golden'. Goldens were characterized by the pinstripe frame and gearcase lining in gold leaf. Sunbeams were very expensive bicycles indeed and, as such, were bought by a privileged clientele. The firm's catalogues and dealers' handbook stressed this and the fact that the Sunbeam was made 'where no second-grade cycles are made'. The company became John Marston Ltd. in March 1895.

In 1899 and 1900, Marston dipped a toe into the motor car market, making two prototypes, neither of which was put into production. Instead, a design was bought in from one M.M. Smith, who had patented his strange four-wheeler in 1900. The Mabley-Sunbeam sold quite well and Marstons went into car production, separating the car company off in 1905, but continuing to 'buy-in' vehicles from Berliet of France, to be modified and sold as Sunbeams. The production of cars at Paul Street had prompted the making of radiators for them – easily done in a sheet-metal factory – and John Marston expanded this side of the business, selling off the domestic japanware side in 1903.

By 1911, Marston was ready to enter another profitable market, that of motor cycles. The 'Gentleman's Motor Cycle' was the result and 'The Sunbeam' was as beautifully finished as the cycles. The 'Royal' and 'Golden' had reached their zenith in the years just before the Great War and were to continue unchanged while the focus of design work shifted to the $2^3/4$ hp and $3^1/2$ hp motor cycles.

Surprisingly perhaps, in view of the firm's image, the early motor cycles were swiftly entered in competition, almost taking the Isle of Man TT on their first appearance in 1914. The Great War put paid to this for a time and the firm was occupied in radiator production whilst making a relatively small number of motor cycles for France, Italy and Russia, and cycles for France.

After the war, the competition use of Sunbeams was intensified in the hands of Alec Bennett, Tommy de la Hay and George Dance, the latter's superb tuning and riding skills pushing Sunbeam to the front of trials and racing. They won the Senior TT four times in the nineteen-twenties.

The company, meanwhile, had changed. John Marston had retired in 1916, dying in 1918, and Marston's was sold, later becoming a part of Nobel Industries. The production of high-grade cycles and motor cycles went on alongside radiators and, in 1928, John Marston Ltd. became part of the new ICI conglomerate.

ICI invested money and bought in new methods, the production being work-studied and rationalised. Out went the hand-soldered craftsmanship and in came bought-in components, tanks, mudguards and gears. In 1937 the cycle and motor cycle business was sold to Associated Motor Cycles of London, already owners of Sunbeam's old Wolverhampton rivals, AJS.

AMC made excellent, though different, Sunbeam cycles and introduced a new range of well-engineered motor cycles. As war again took over, these were discontinued and AMC made WD motor cycles 'for the duration'. (John Marston Ltd. was wound up in 1943, becoming Marston Excelsior in amalgamation with the Excelsior Motor Radiator Co. of Leeds, later becoming I.M.I.-Marston Ltd. and then Marston-Palmer Ltd., still in Wolverhampton).

In 1943 AMC sold the Sunbeam trademarks to BSA of Birmingham, who produced 'war-grade' Sunbeam cycles from that date. In 1946 a new Sunbeam motor cycle appeared, to be followed in 1959 by two motor-scooters.

In 1956–7 the cycle interests were sold to Raleigh of Nottingham who, inexplicably, discontinued BSA's nicely-made touring Sunbeam cycles and transferred the famous trademark to a range of children's 'pavement cycles'.

At the time of writing, the future of the motor cycle trademark is in doubt, following the re-structuring of Norton-Villiers-Triumph, successors to the BSA group. The cycle rights remain with Raleigh Industries.

This book covers almost exactly a century of the Sunbeam trademark, under which name the finest cycles ever made were sold, as well as some of the most fondly-remembered motor cycles.

Acknowledgements

In addition to Jacqueline, James and Gemma, the author wishes to thank the others who have so willingly helped in the production of this book. In particular, Marston Palmer Ltd., Melissa Marston, John Pinkerton, Bob Currie, Christopher Deanesly, Jean Rumsey, Walter Iliff and the others, whose names appear inside.

Walsall, England
Saintes, France

Robert Cordon Champ
August 1988

A note about the photographs

Where possible, the photographs in this book are both contemporary and unpublished. The only exceptions to this are where only one photograph of a particular subject is known and a decision not to use it would result in a noticeable gap. All of the catalogue-style photographs are original 'works' ones which escaped the wholesale destruction of archive material from Sunbeams which took place in 1937, 1940 – when, for instance, Sidney Bowers sent all of his Sunbeam material to the waste paper 'drive' – and 1971–2 when BSA was cleared out. Two major 'private' contributions are from George Dance's own photograph album and that of Sidney Bowers.

All such photographs, as well as those from the Marston Palmer collection, are acknowledged, whilst unacknowledged photographs are from the author's collection.

One of a series taken outside the Paul Street Works on 18th August 1888, this is the earliest known photograph of Sunbeams. The machine on the left, held by Charles Marston, is of the cross-frame safety type, common at the time. John Marston is holding a tricycle also of a then usual type. No catalogues for these machines have been found to date but the cycle appears identical to the sketches of Sunbeams published in the contemporary press.

The photograph survived by being passed down in the family of Sidney Bowers, who rose from apprentice to Managing Director of John Marston Ltd.   *(Photo: Ted Manley)*

This diamond-frame model, new for 1892, was the first Sunbeam fitted with Harrison Carter's patent chain case to be catalogued. This was a non-detachable, oil-bath container soldered to the frame which both protected and lubricated the chain. At first offered as an extra, Carter's case became the 'Sunbeam Carter Chain Case' in 1894, later the 'Sunbeam Chain Case', gaining the famous name of 'Sunbeam Little Oil Bath' in 1897, a phrase which became indelibly linked with Sunbeams.

Opposite page top: **An advertising keepsake from John Marston Ltd., this brass and ceramic ashtray dates from 1892.**

Opposite page bottom: **The splendid hat complements a Ladies' 'Royal' model of 1899 or 1900, priced at £21.10s. when new. The 'Royal' has seen some service and has been fitted with a rear brake indicating a conversion from fixed to free-wheel. The finish is typically early Sunbeam with nickelled fork-ends and fittings.**

'Gracious, I am nearly mad with joy – it's a Sunbeam with Dunlop tyres' (Winifred Llewhellin's diary – March 1896)

(Photo: J.E.N. Pinkerton)

From 1903 Marstons offered the silent and elegant epicyclic two-speed gear mounted inside the front chainwheel. From 1907, a modified version was combined with a Sunbeam three-speed to provide the 'Golden' Model A6 with six speeds.

Sunbeams also offered a rear hub two-speed made by The Villiers Cycle Components Company, set up by John Marston to make cycle components and run by Charles Marston from 1898 to 1946.

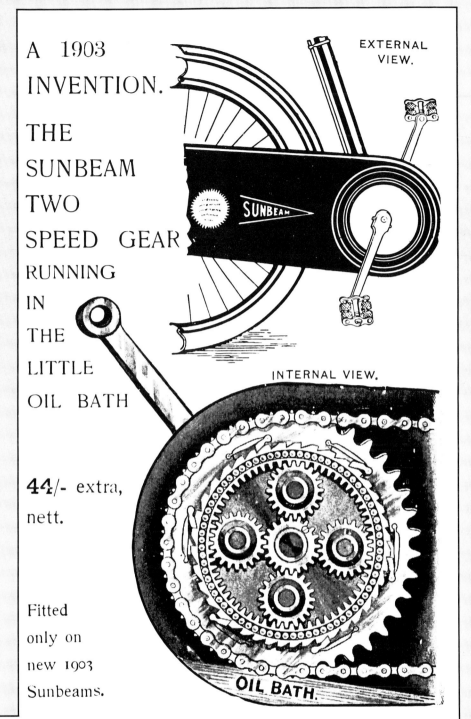

A 1903 INVENTION.

THE SUNBEAM TWO SPEED GEAR RUNNING IN THE LITTLE OIL BATH

EXTERNAL VIEW.

SUNBEAM

INTERNAL VIEW.

OIL BATH.

44/- extra, nett.

Fitted only on new 1903 Sunbeams.

DESCRIPTION OF TWO SPEED GEAR

This Two-Speed Gear is fixed inside the crank chain wheel of the Royal Sunbeam Bicycle. It is thus entirely enclosed by our dust-proof oil tight gear case, and its mechanism runs in the little oil bath.

The change of gear from one speed to the other is effected by moving a small hand lever affixed to the frame, and connected by means of a flexible wire with the small central cog of the gearing. When this central cog is held stationary the high gear is obtained, when it is loose, and so allowed to revolve round with the other small cogs, the low gear.

Cleanliness of surroundings and perfect lubrication tend to prevent friction from the gear teeth. The more important part of the mechanism is also mounted on ball bearings.

It is noteworthy that the ball free wheel on the hub is undisturbed by this gear, so riders will not find their friends outcoast them down slopes, as is often the case with bicycles where the two-speed mechanism is combined with the free wheel in the rear hub.

The following choice of gears can at present be supplied:

High Set (82 and 66).   Medium Set (78 and 62).

Low Set (74 and 59).   Ladies' Set (66 and 53).

'Sunbeam Variations'
Dr. (later Sir) Edward Elgar owned more than one Sunbeam, ordering his final one, shown here, in February 1903.
Elgar was 5ft 10 in and rode 'Mr. Phoebus', a 28 in Royal fitted with three brakes, for some years, often with Dora
Penny. ('Dorabella', Variation 10 of 'The Enigma Variations' Opus 36.) His older 'Mr. Phoebus', a 1900 27 in Royal
was given to his music publisher, August Jaeger ('Nimrod' Variation No. 9)   *(Photo: The Elgar Foundation.)*

Elgar, the future Master of the King's Musick, is seen here cycling with the Malverns in the background. It was
considered gentlemanly to ride a tall cycle, a tradition with which the writer concurs. (Elgar was Enigma Variation
14, 'EDU'). His musical version of a puncture was:

'Ought I to buy new ones (tyres) or will these last without

 ing for a few more months?'

8   *(Photo: The Elgar Foundation.)*

John Marston and Ellen Marston in about 1905.

(Photo: Melissa Marston)

One feature of the cycles which carried on to the motor cycles was the use of a divided axle and spacer on the rear wheel to enable a deflated tube to be taken out for repair without removing the wheel or chain drive. It was purchased by Marston's from its inventor, Archibald Sharp, and was used on motor cycles into the mid-twenties and somewhat later on cycles. In both cases, the major problem was not of getting the tyre or tube past the hub but of having to disconnect the rear brake, a problem which Sunbeams wisely forgot to mention!

TYRE REMOVAL

WITHOUT DISTURBING THE GEAR CASE OR DRIVING BEARINGS.

This Patent System, invented by Professor Sharp, the well-known Cycle Engineer, has been purchased for the exclusive use of Sunbeam Riders.

In 1899 and 1900 John Marston Ltd. made two prototype motor cars. These needed radiators and this new line of sheet metal work became the mainstay of the Paul Street Works for the future and still is for their successors in 1988. This is a 1907 advertisement. One of the John Marston Ltd. customers was the Sunbeam Motor Company formed in 1905 to make Sunbeam cars in Upper Villiers St.

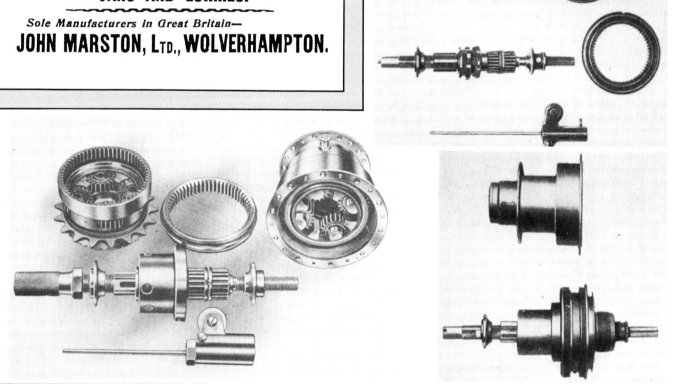

In 1907 Sunbeams listed a three-speed gear in a 'stepped' rear hub. Fitted with a silent free-wheel, this complex and expensive device was replaced from 1913 by a cheaper hub with a cylindrical case, almost identical to that of the contemporary BSA. Sunbeam gears were made at 'The Villiers', later prolific makers of motor cycle and industrial engines.

The three-speed 'Golden' Sunbeam could be obtained in black and nickel or all-black finish from 1913. In either case, the frame lining was done in real gold leaf, for Sunbeams never used gold paint. An example of a product made deliberately to the highest standards, the pre-1918 Sunbeam is undoubtedly the finest production cycle ever made.

The design was to be in production for fifty years in the hands of four different companies.

(Photo: Marston Palmer)

Sunbeam's first motor cycle was this neat Stevens-designed 75 x 79 mm $2^1/2$ hp (349 cc) side-valve single. A prominent feature was the use of Oil Bath Chain Cases for primary and secondary drives. In fact, this was a misnomer, for the motor cycle rear chain cases were never oil containers in the way that the bicycle ones were. At first, the tank was painted in the Sunbeam cycle's Olive Green, with silver panels, but this was soon replaced with black enamel and gold-leaf lining.

A Gentleman's Motor Cycle.

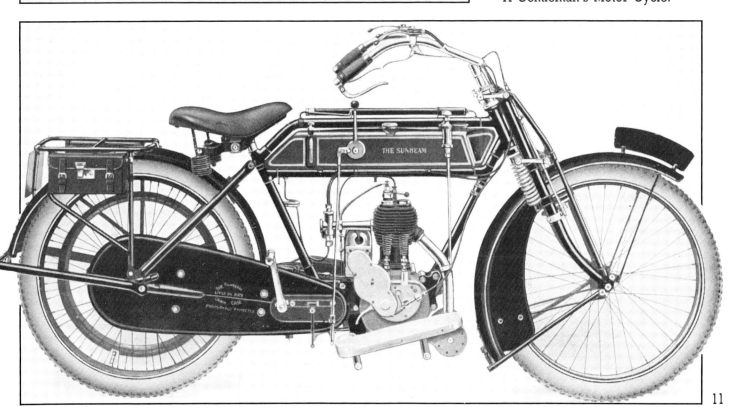

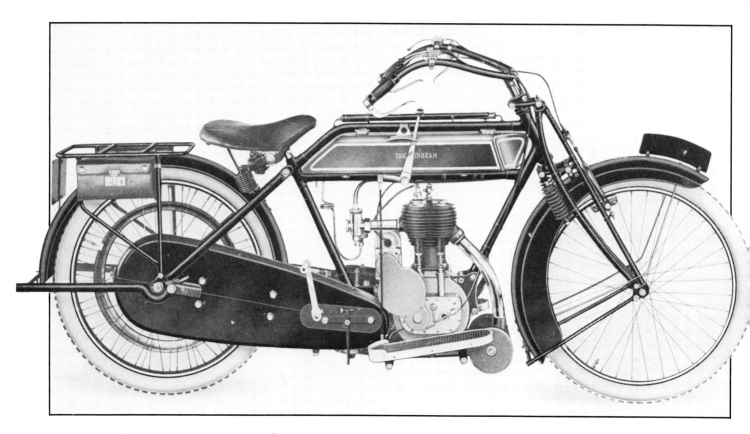

The second Sunbeam design was of $3^1/2$ hp, an 85 x 88 mm single with a three-speed gearbox, an altogether more robust motor cycle than the dainty $2^3/4$. This was entirely the work of John Marston's new designer and chief engineer, John Ernest Greenwood MIAE. Born in Dewsbury, Yorkshire, on 27th March, 1873, John Greenwood joined Marston's in 1911 and designed almost every engine until 1933. His '$3^1/2$' stayed in production until 1926. The large bulge on the timing case contains the central magneto drive gear wheel, the mark of a pre-1915 Sunbeam.

An optimistic view of the Sunbeamland factory from the 1914 catalogue. The factory still stands at the junction of Paul Street and Pool Street with Jeddo Street and the original Jeddo Works behind.

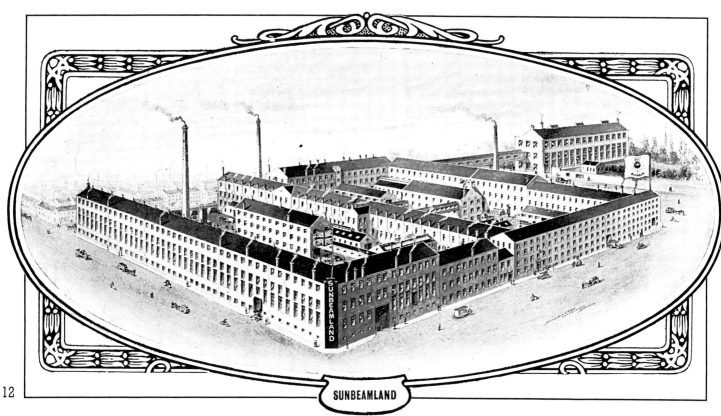

SUNBEAMLAND

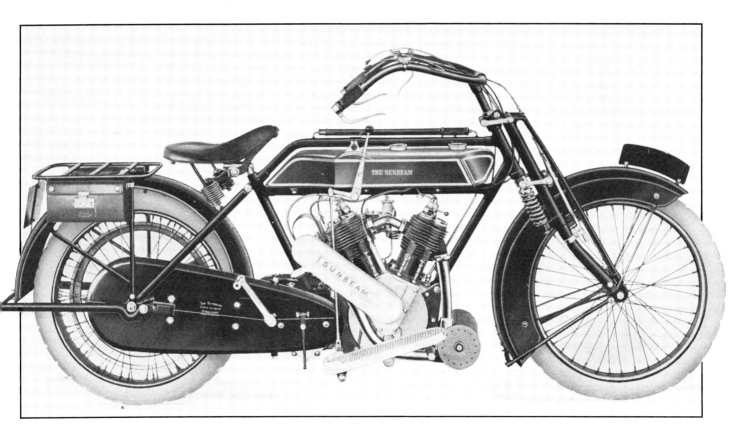

Sunbeams also made a V-twin machine for the sidecar market. This 1914 version used a 770 cc engine by J.A. Prestwich of London with a three-speed gearbox of Sunbeam's own make, as was the multiple plate clutch. The partisan work force of Paul Street regarded these machines as being only 'half a Sunbeam' because of the proprietary engine. They were finished in the same way as contemporary Sunbeam cycles, with all links, controls and adjustable fittings nickel plated.

A familiar but charming photograph, this shows the 'works' demonstrator DA 1348, a JAP 6 hp twin fitted with a 'Gloria' boat-shaped cane body, in 1913. There is a large leather case on the carrier and the outfit looks well-used, the absence of fresh road dirt on the rider suggesting that she had not been long in the saddle. The sidecar mudguard is box-lined, cycle-fashion, though Sunbeam never lined mudguards, chaincases and handlebars on motor cycles.

Vernon Busby was the AMAC carburettor representative who rode competitively for Sunbeams before the Great War and is now almost forgotten. Here he is in March 1914 in rural France on the Paris – Nice reliability trial, on a 1914 pattern $3^1/2$ hp DA 226. The painted advertisement is for Ducellier headlamps and it would not be difficult to find a similar level-crossing background in France today.

Another French background for Busby in the same trial. He won a Gold Medal and the Prince of Monaco's Prize. Either this shot was taken in northern France or the southern weather was bad enough to warrant his heavy paramatta suit. He was killed flying in 1918.

Left to right, Howard Davies, Tommy de la Hay and Vernon Busby line up for the 1914 TT – Sunbeam's first – in a Douglas photographer's studio.

The machines were rather special versions of the $3\frac{1}{2}$ hp with two brakes on the rear wheel. The registration numbers DA 1494, DA 1495 and AB 3501 appear on 'works' Sunbeams throughout the nineteen-twenties. MN 496 is a local Isle of Man registration.

H.R. Davies rode brilliantly to get second place in his and Sunbeam's first TT race. His fastest lap was 45.13 mph. After the war he rode for AJS, Sunbeam's Wolverhampton rivals, and then made his own HRD machines in Wolverhampton, finished, like AJS and Sunbeam, in black and gold.

Auto-Cycle Union

CERTIFICATE OF PERFORMANCE

(No. 12).

UNDER THE OPEN COMPETITION RULES OF THE A·C·U·

Senior International Auto-Cycle Tourist Trophy Race

1914.

This is to certify that each of the team of three 3½ h.p. Sunbeam Motorbicycles entered by Messrs. John Marston Limited, of Wolverhampton for the Senior International Auto-Cycle Tourist Trophy Race, held in the Isle of Man on 21st May 1914, successfully completed the course of 225 miles within thirty minutes of the time taken by the winner of the Race, and accomplished the best performance of the 17 teams entered.

Particulars of the individual performances are as follows :—

Driver	Motorcycle.	Bore.	Stroke	c.c.	Position at finish of Race.	Total Time.
H. R. Davies	Sunbeam	83	88	500	2nd.	4 hr. 39 m. 12 s.
V. Busby	"	"	"	"	11th.	4 hr. 56 m. 3 s.
T. C. de la Hay	"	"	"	"	13th.	4 hr. 57 m. 20 s.

Percy Greenwell
Chairman of Competitions Committee.

T. Loughborough
Secretary.

83, Pall Mall.
London, S.W.

After Charlie Nokes became ill in practice, Sunbeams substituted their reserve, Thomas Corbett de la Hay. H.R. Davies came in 2nd, Vernon Busby 11th and Tommy de la Hay 13th. Sunbeams had won the team prize, but the ACU awarded it to Rovers on the grounds that the Sunbeam team was not the one named in their entry. A tremendous row ensued, the ACU caved in and the trophy went to Wolverhampton, where ACU remained a dirty word for years.

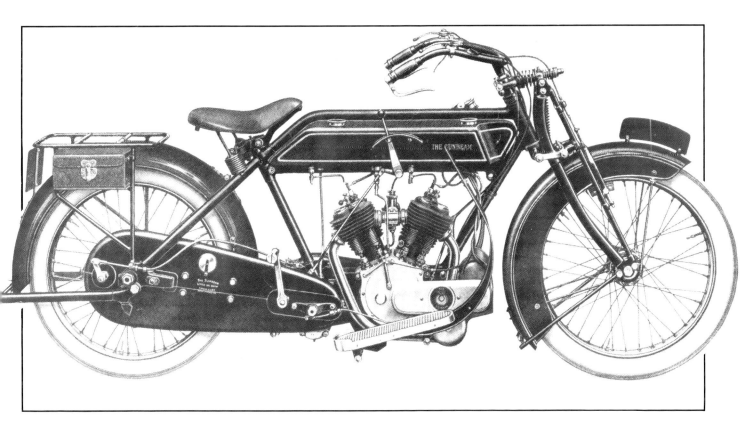

The J.A. Prestwich V-twin engine in the 1914 6 hp Sunbeam was succeeded by an AKD one for the 1915 season. Abingdon King Dick are more famous for their hand tools – which Marstons used as they did their tricycle axles – and their trademark is the British Bulldog. The 798 cc engine lasted in the catalogue for one season only.

The beautiful 3^1/$_2$ hp Sunbeam was lightly redesigned for 1915 while the 2^3/$_4$ hp was dropped.

    Changes included an excellent new gearbox and magneto drive by an immensely strong Coventry inverted-tooth chain. The finish was that which had become standard on the bicycles, the so-called 'All-Black' style, where the amount of nickel was decreased. (An example in the hands of the author has, however, an almost 1914 style black and nickel finish).

Four small photographs on opposite page: A selection of Great War pictures. 3^1/$_2$ hp and 8 hp Sunbeams were used by the governments of England, France, Italy and Russia, in both WD green and black and gold finishes. Machines in use in England are shown with OHMS on the front number-plate.

Opposite page bottom: The original caption to this photograph says 'Soldier cyclists on Silent Sunbeams'. It is dated 1914, the unit is the 25th City of London Territorial Reserve Battalion, and the cycles are civilian models with rifle clips for the Enfield rifles.

Below Right: A solid, trouble-free gearbox, this rack and pinion operated three-speed was introduced for the 1915 season. It was designed and made at Sunbeamland in line with John Marston's policy of making all possible components at the works in order to maintain control over specification and quality. This type of gearbox was fitted to 3^1/$_2$, 4^1/$_4$ and 8 hp models and was used until 1932 on the Model 7. A modernised version then became standard until 1935.

'The Military Sunbeam' was made in quantity for the French Government and also sold in small numbers in England. There was a minor fashion during the war for buying goods in military style both to send out to relatives in the forces or for home use both by soldiers and by civilians, this latter presumably as an expression of solidarity. This machine was a standard Sunbeam without an oilbath, finished in WD green and with Joseph Lucas rifle clips and a front carrier, the rear one being charged as an extra.

One of the photographs signed by John Marston on May 6 1916 when he relinquished day to day control of
20 Sunbeamland.

Presumably shortages of JAP engines in 1916 made Marstons use the Swiss Motosacoche AG 2C9 twin inlet over exhaust motor. An inelegant machine whose looks could have been markedly improved by placing the magneto behind the cylinder. Most went to the Czar's forces though some were sold on the civilian market.

After Marston's death, a tablet was placed in St. Peter's Church, Wolverhampton. It says:

To the Greater Glory of God and to the memory of John Marston. Twice Mayor of Wolverhampton. An Alderman and Freeman of the Borough and Justice of the Peace. Died March 8th 1918. Aged 81 years. He developed the whole cycle, motor cycle and motor-car industry and he was a just and honourable employer. His integrity, public spirit and Christian faith made him an example to all. This tablet is erected by the employees at Sunbeamland the factory he owned for nearly fifty years.

(Photo: Christopher Deanesly)

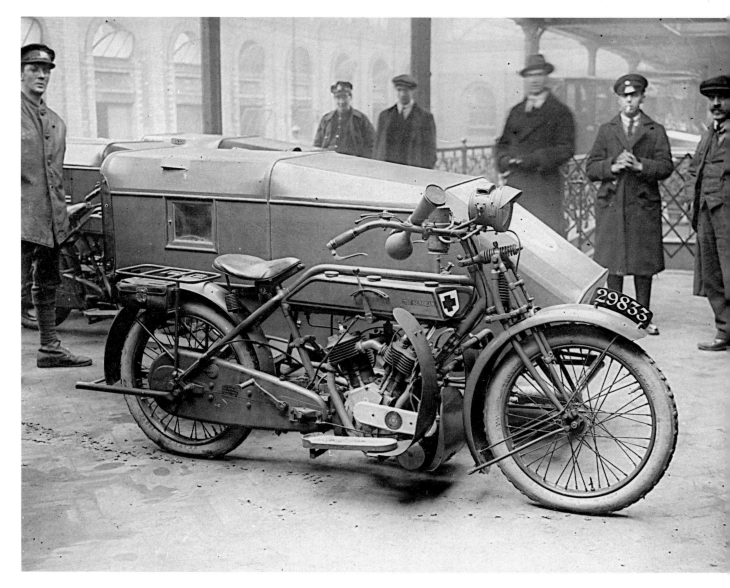

An 8 hp JAP-engined ambulance stretcher-carrying outfit sold as surplus after the war. This is the second version, the earlier ones having merely a modified sidecar chassis with a folding pram-type hood at the front to protect the hapless casualty's head. On this, the later model, the front of the sidecar had two holes through which the stretcher handles protruded.

An experimental Sunbeam outfit with sprung rear frame and sidecar wheel on test in Wales in August 1919. The driver is W. Norman Bowkett, MIMechE, who was chief draughtsman at John Marston Ltd., from 1915 to 1931, when he was appointed Chief Engineer, succeeding John Greenwood.

Sunbeams, wrote Bowkett, 'were designed and manufactured up to the highest standard of precision engineering and not, like many competitors, down to a price.'

John Greenwood was a hard rider at speed trials and is seen here with one of his daughters in the sidecar of DA 1349. In 1919, at Style Cop, near Rugeley in Staffordshire, the pair had a fearsome smash when John turned the outfit over. Despite 'clothes badly torn and a badly cut head, and with his passenger very much shaken' the pair rode home to Wolverhampton in the Sunbeam.

The Victory Cup Trial took place at Easter in 1919. Here is Eddie Kickham attacking the Malvern Hills' Wyche Cutting. His outfit has the then novel electric lighting but a very basic sidecar.

The Sunbeam riders for the 1920 Senior TT. Left to right Frank Townshend, George Dance, Tommy de la Hay, Reg Brown, a mechanic, John Greenwood and Eric Williams.

In the race Dance left the whole field for dead, setting two record laps and leading by over three minutes until his inlet valve broke on the last lap, the first of a whole series of TT retirements for George. de la Hay came through to win, with Reg Brown third and Frank Townshend ninth. *(Photo: The Dance Collection)*

Tommy de la Hay (60) overtaking N.C. Sclater, Norton, at Craig-ny-Baa in the 1920 Senior TT. Sitting on a wall to watch the race is one aspect of the TT which hasn't changed in over sixty years.

Two leading motorcycle designers of the 1920s, John Greenwood and James L. Norton, photographed after the 1920 TT.

The greatest sprint rider of the 1920s was George Dance, who had joined Marston's from market gardening and steam engines in 1914. He quickly established a reputation as a fine tester and tuner – albeit by 'rule of thumb' methods – whose aversion to anything like paperwork was legendary. A quiet, taciturn man of phenomenal physical strength, Dance came alive on a sprint motor cycle and had a reputation for winning every class at public road sprints. Here he sits on a 1921 TT Sunbeam. *(Photo: The Dance Collection)*

Opposite page top: **George Dance out in the country in a trial in 1920.** *(Photo: The Dance Collection)*

Opposite page bottom: **A close-up of the 1921 works racer showing the frame-mounted oil-tank whose sight-feed** was cable operated by the rear of the two pedals. The front one was for the rear brake. Oil from the feed went to the mechanical pump and was then distributed round the engine. The photograph shows the lovely enamel and immaculate nickel plate contrasting with the matt-finished engine castings. The effect of muted quality is often ruined by present-day 'restorers' who polish Sunbeam castings.

Alec Bennett on the 85 x 88 mm racer after the 1921 Senior TT. New for the racers was the mechanical oiling system by the rider's boot. The Sunbeams did not win, de la Hay retiring with a blown valve cap and Dance, jammed in top gear after a crash, finished eighth for his only TT Replica. Bennett was fourth.

(Photo: Marston Palmer)

Alec Bennett after winning the 1921 French Grand Prix. This was the first appearance of Greenwood's demon new 'Longstroke' engine, so-called because of its piston stroke of 105.5 mm compared to the bore of 77 mm. The finest side-valve engine ever made by Marston's it stayed in production until 1940. Bennett won at 59.9 mph average speed.

A snapshot taken immediately after the finish of the French G.P. Bennett had won and de la Hay, on the left, was second.

The road surface may be noticed, contributing to the caked mud on Bennett's Sunbeam on the posed picture. The man assisting de la Hay with his crash helmet may well be Albert Tonks, later the chief race fitter.

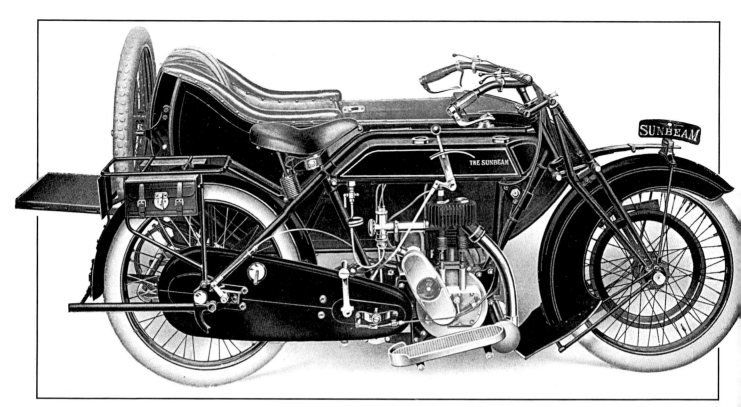

Opposite page top: For the 1922 Season, Sunbeams did the logical thing and combined the 105.5 mm stroke Longstroke with the 85 mm bore 3 $\frac{1}{2}$ hp giving an engine capacity of 596 cc. The 'Model 7' or 4$\frac{1}{4}$ hp was a splendid 'slogger' which pulled great weights and lasted seemingly for ever. It remained in production well into the nineteen-thirties, the last 'flat-tank' motorcycle to be produced by a major factory.

Opposite page bottom: George giving it full throttle. 'Go or bust' was his motto and go or bust he did, astounding opponents on occasion by taking every class, solo and sidecar, at sprint meetings. This may be Clipstone Park.

(Photo: The Dance Collection)

George Dance pouring in the Castrol at a sprint meeting. Bert Tetstall is in the chair and the machine is a sprinter based on an 85 x 88 mm 1915-pattern engine. The car at rear is believed to be George's Cubitt tourer which was his race transport.

(Photo: The Dance Collection) 31

Nett Price—
£26 0 0

INCLUDING FREE WHEEL,
SUNBEAM TWO-SPEED
GEAR,
AND THE LITTLE OIL
BATH.

Another Dance combination, based on a 1914 2³/4, this has vertical overhead valves. The faithful Tetstall is in the sidecar, the whole surrounded by a noble array of hats. *(Photo: The Dance Collection)*

The Golden Sunbeam Tricycle was charmingly advertised as being most suitable for 'nervous and elderly riders'.

It ran from 1907 until the later 1920s but was only made to order. The rear axle was supplied complete by Abingdon King Dick and contained a differential and band brake.

Taken in Europe this sunny picture has Tommy de la Hay and George Dance mounted on pre-production overhead-valve Sunbeams in the early 1920s.

(Photo: The Dance Collection)

But later the weather got wet . . .

(Photo: The Dance Collection)

Eddie Small on the way to the Scottish ACU's Hillclimb at Walgram Brae. The car is an ABC flat-twin tourer, the bike a George Dance replica based on a 1914 2³/₄ hp.

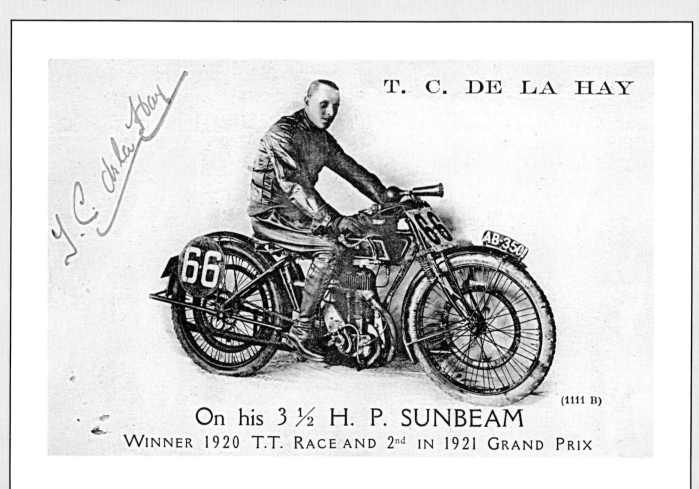

T. C. DE LA HAY

(1111 B)

On his 3 ½ H. P. SUNBEAM
WINNER 1920 T.T. RACE AND 2nd IN 1921 GRAND PRIX

T. C. DE LA-HAY.
SENIOR T. T. RACE. 1921.

Photographs on this and opposite page bottom: **Three shots of Sunbeam's faithful rider, Tommy de la Hay, protégé of Sid Bowers, the works manager.**

The signature decorates a Sunbeam publicity postcard, the action shot is the 1921 Senior TT, and the third one a 1925 posed publicity photograph.

(Photos: Marston Palmer)

Opposite page top: Ernesto Vailati re-fuelling in the 1922 Italian TT on an early overhead-valve Sunbeam. He survived petrol dripping on to a red-hot engine and went on to win in record time.

Vailati was the Sunbeam importer for Italy and a popular figure there and at Sunbeamland.

(Photo: The Bowers Collection)

Opposite page bottom: Vailati again, on a standard 'Longstroke' racer in 1922, in an era when Italian riders were proud to wear 'Sunbeam' on their sweaters. The rim front brake on this model was famous for its lack of stopping power but that mattered little to some racing men.

(Photo: The Bowers Collection)

The British stand at the 1923 Oslo Motor Show, with Sunbeam's Longstroke 'Grand Prix Racer' showing off its fine finish and toolkit (with spare cams). The road machine stands behind.

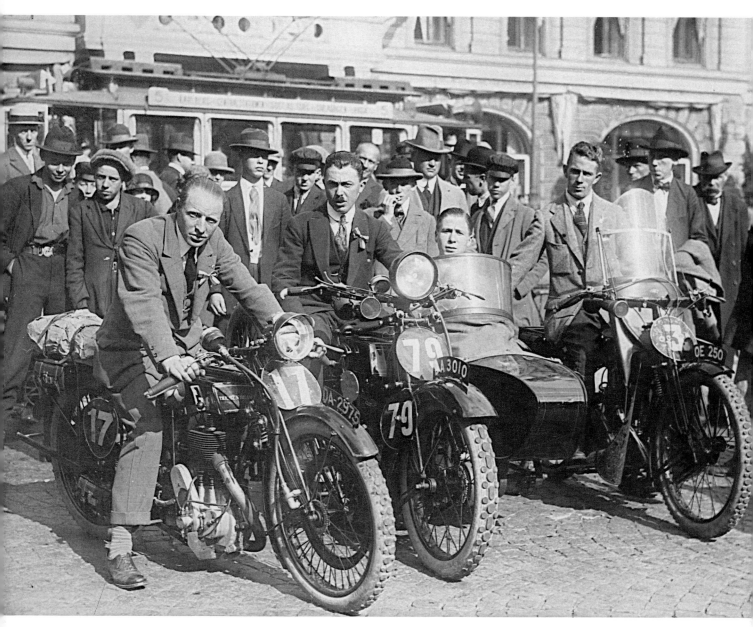

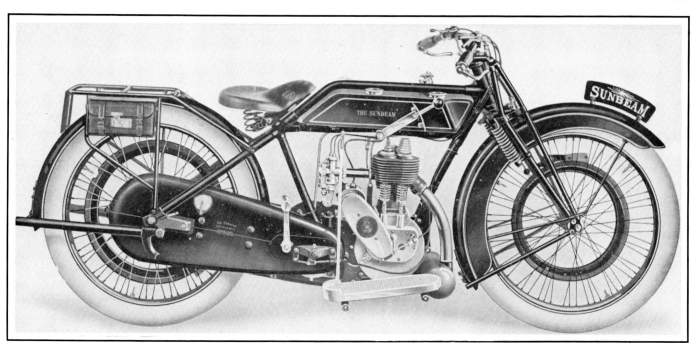

38

Opposite page top: Tommy de la Hay astride a Longstroke next to Frank Giles, as ever, AJS-mounted, in Oslo. Bert Kershaw (Omega) is on their left.

Opposite page bottom: A re-introduction for 1923 was a 350 cc, or $2^3/4$ hp machine, a capacity neglected by the works since 1914. A fairly mundane machine, its significance was that its design acted as the basis for all of Sunbeam's overhead-valve road and race machines into the 1930s.

George Dance on an overhead-valve sprinter at the Chatcombe start line, near Cheltenham, in 1924. The great width of the handlebars enabled Dance to hold the bucking sprinter on the rough roads.

Although one or two supposed 'Dance' sprinters have been exhibited, none is authenticated. In any case, engines and frames were swapped around to suit the event.

(Photo: The Dance Collection) 39

Achille Varzi was an absolutely top-class Italian rider who became one of the great Grand Prix car drivers. He is seated on a 1924 pattern 'Sprint' Sunbeam, developed by Dance for the public-road sprints and hill-climbs current in Europe and England. The engine's straight-through porting system necessitated a split front down-tube to accommodate the exhaust system, while the wedge tank held enough for a few miles only, the whole a production version of a George Dance special, made from 1924 to 1926.

(Photo: Marston Palmer)

The 1925 Model Longstroke 'speedman's machine'. Fitted now with drum brakes – if pretty small ones – this style of machine was the high point of the 'motor bicycle'. As the 'twenties progressed, weight and complexity crept in. If you can, try to ride one of these to taste the magic of a great design.

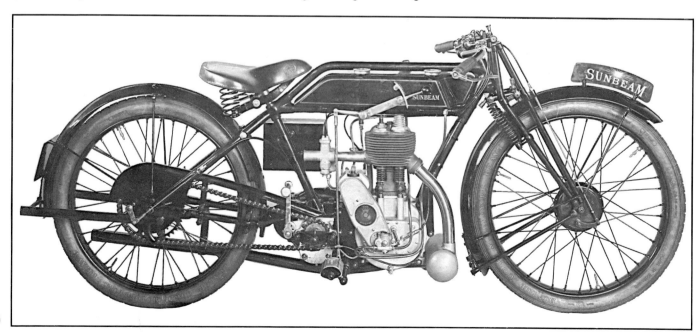

George Dance and Mrs. Dance on yet another re-incarnation of DA 1494 in 1921.

(Photo: The Dance Collection)

Right thumb on the open throttle lever, George Dance hits the start line at Harling sprint in 1923, clutch not fully home and rear wheel just starting to spin.

(Photo: The Dance Collection)

It is the 26th February 1924 and F. Gyr, Rosenbaum, Jack Woodhouse and H. Gyr are posed at the control of the Deutschlandfahrt in Berlin, a trial of over 2500 miles. Gyr's machine is a 3½ hp, Woodhouse's a 4¼ hp, 'mit beiwagen'. The two riders and machines won Best Solo and Best Sidecar. As Marston's gleefully pointed out, they were 'the only two Sunbeams in the trial'.

(Photo: The Bowers Collection)

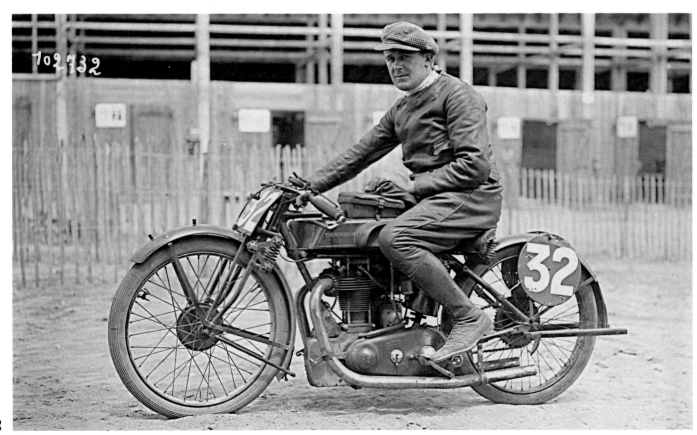

Photographs on this and opposite page bottom: Seemingly the only contemporary shot of the company's 1925 foray into overhead-camshaft engines. Alec Jackson is seen at the 1925 French GP. Designed by Greenwood, with oil tank in the sump, the engine was not successful, owing to a lack of knowledge about, and research on, the new cam profiles needed. It was noisy, known at the works as the 'Crocodile' because, like its namesake who swallowed the clock in 'Peter Pan', it went 'tick-tock', in contrast to the quietness required of a Sunbeam. Two survive, one of which is now in the Haynes Sparkford Motor Museum as illustrated in the accompanying two photographs, but Greenwood's invention and patent of the 'hairpin' valve spring went on, becoming standard on racing Sunbeams and, much later, AMC machines.

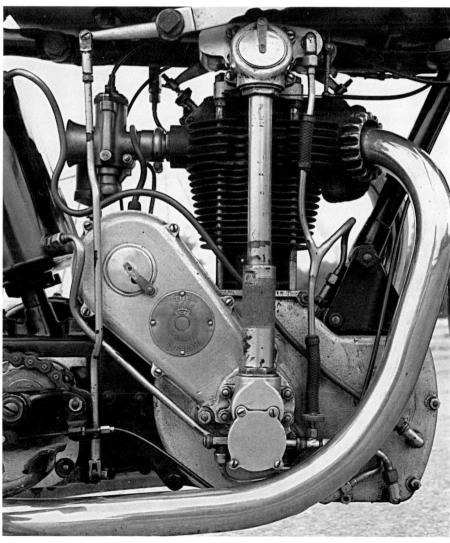

Conditions in Sunbeamland were much the same as in any other engineering works of the 1920s. The company was always a strict employer but paid good wages and had a long tradition of sons and daughters joining fathers to work at 'The Sunbeam'.

Dr. Paul Feledy, a noted Hungarian rider and winner of the 1925 Austrian TT, is seen here on an overhead-valve racer, its condition reflecting the muddy or dusty conditions found in races at the time. The machine is basically a Model II 493 cc 'Sprint' but with an altered, large-capacity tank. *(Photo: Marston Palmer)*

From Italy, a super group photograph. From left to right, Graham Walker (in white shirt), Ernesto Vailati, Tommy de la Hay, George Dance, Achille Varzi, an unknown, Albert Collins (Sunbeam's race fitter), two unknown people and, far right, Angelo Varzi.

The machines are c.1927 works specials in the 'Sprint' tradition but fitted with two-port engines and the optional taper tanks with rounded fronts, and separate oil tanks.

French Bol d'Or winner, Monsieur F. Francisquet astride his 1926 '500' racer with 'George Dance' kneegrips, obligatory wear for the discerning speedman. Though having a two-port head, the frame is that of the earlier, split down-tube type, illustrating the fact that most competition machines were 'bitzas'.

Swiss rider, Monsieur Ruche, photographed in Geneva, on a 1926 'parallel' Model 9, so-called because it was a road-going version of the 'Sprint' but with parallel frame and top tubes.

1928 Reliance Cup winner, Harold Fearnside, on an interesting 'works' trials special, basically an overhead-valve 'parallel'. Noteworthy are the early high-level exhaust system, race-style Bentley & Draper front dampers and the 'bobby-dodger' lights. A 26 x 2½ x 2¼ in beaded edge tyre serves on the front, but the 26 x 3 in voiturette section tyre hasn't protected the rear rim from a hefty dent. The rider is clean and polished, suggesting a 'day-after' photo at Alec Jackson's depot.

The days when a motorcycle was light and slim. The hot-stuff 500 cc overhead-valve Sunbeam with twin-port engine for 1927. Two exhaust ports on a two-valve head was a contemporary fashion. Controls pictured from left to right of picture are valve lifter, throttle (lower), air lever (upper), hand gear change, magneto advance/retard, clutch, front brake (always on the *left* bar on vintage Sunbeams). The only foot control is that for the rear brake, on the right of the picture.

48

The machines for the 1926 TT were Sunbeam's first serious use of the 'saddle tank', later to become universal in motor cycling. This development, where the top rail of the frame was hidden by the enveloping tank, caught on in a big way in 1928-9. Otherwise the TT machines differed from the 1925 ones in a return to a push-rod overhead valve engine, and the use of eight-inch brakes, a huge size for their day. Normality returned for 1927.

Works rider and tester Tommy Deadman on his road special, utilising parts from the 1926 works TT models, which were broken up or sold after their lack of success. Sic transit gloria ......

(Photo: Tommy Deadman) 49

Graham Walker in his final year as competition gaffer at Marstons, Charles J.P. Dodson, the new signing for 1927 and Lancastrian Walter Lees (Dick) Birch, a founder member of the TT Riders Association, span the highway in a photographer's studio after the 1927 TT. Walker finished 5th, Dodson 8th and Birch 16th, netting the Manufacturer's Team Prize for the first time since 1914. Former Sunbeam rider Alec Bennett won the race on a Norton. Sartorially correct, Walker sports two cycle saddle-bags on his belt (for pipe and matches, no doubt).

Opposite page top: Luigi Arcangeli at the start of the 1927 Grand Prix des Nations which he won. Interestingly, on the back of the print was a note requesting a passport photograph for Dodson from Sunbeam's own photographer. On Arcangeli's right, mounted on a dohc 350cc Bianchi, is Italy's most famous racing driver of all, Tazio Nuvolari. He won the 350cc class.

Opposite page bottom: The Models 80 and 90 and their 'alter egos', the works racers, had a new-style tank for 1928, with a rounded front end which was given the nickname of 'bullnose'. This is Dodson's Junior TT mount for that year, UK 5225, with the short 'Dodson' saddle. The engine features Greenwood's hairpin springs.

50   In the race all the Sunbeams, ridden by Dodson, Arcangeli, Franconi, Emery and Major, retired or crashed.

Looking apprehensive, Ernie Mainwaring on a 498 cc Scott lines up on the left of Francesco Franconi and of Milan's Luigi Arcangeli for the 1928 Senior. Mainwaring's Scott failed to finish, as it did every year from 1925–1930, whilst Franconi was placed 7th and Arcangeli 15th.

Opposite page top: In the 264 mile 1928 Senior TT Marston's fielded Luigi Arcangeli, Franconi, Dodson and Arthur Simcock, respectively Italian, Swiss, English and Australian!

A Mancunian, C.J.P. Dodson was very small and light, itself worth several horsepower and, more importantly, very good in wet conditions. The race was run in rain which suited him. Here he is, in second gear (out of three), at Hillberry on June 8th, 1928. *(Photo: Marston Palmer)*

Opposite page bottom: So bad were the conditions, with mist and rain, that many riders were seen to be 'footing'. Here is Dodson doing just that at Creg-ny-Baa on Lap 6. Dodson crashed on Lap 6 at Keppel Gate, breaking his rear stand, and losing the lead to Graham Walker, now with Rudge. The Rudge failed ten miles from the finish and 52 Dodson came through to win. Arcangeli was 15th and Franconi 7th, thus gaining Sunbeams the Team Prize.

It is the last lap, after Dodson's big fall, as he negotiates Ramsey Hairpin in perhaps the first pictured example of 'knee-out' cornering. The battered number plate, mudguard and trailing remains of the rear stand can be seen.

Opposite page top: Greenwood and Dodson, in the Paddock after the race, the bike showing all-over evidence of the poor conditions and of the crash at front and rear. The trailing stand caused Dodson to tumble a second time, fortunately without injury. He was to lose his life on a similar Sunbeam giving a demonstration ride in old age.

Opposite page: A Sunbeam publicity postcard, signed by Charlie Dodson, commemorating what was to be the last TT win on a 'flat-tanker' motor cycle.

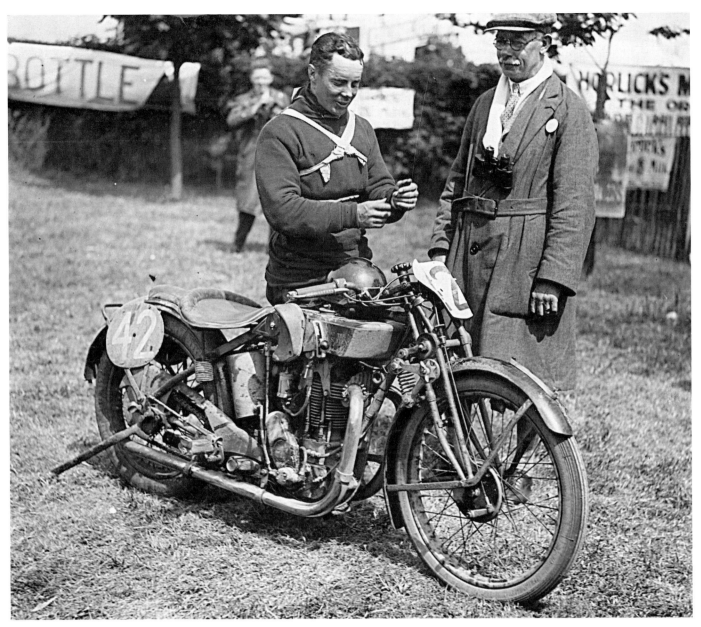

THE SENIOR T.T. RACE WON FOR THE THIRD TIME ON A SUNBEAM.

Mr C.J.P. DODSON, WINNER OF THE 1928 SENIOR T.T. RACE ON HIS MODEL 90 SUNBEAM.

By Courtesy of

Yours sincerely,
C.J.P. Dodson.

Makers:- John Marston Limited, Sunbeamland, Wolverhampton.

Opposite page top: Switzerland's Francesco Franconi, who was a race and hill-climb hard man in Europe, here in his first Senior TT, cornering at Signpost Corner. He finished 7th, taking the Visitors' Prize. *(Photo: Marston Palmer)*

Opposite page bottom: A formidable rider in England was Gordon Cobbold. He specialized in Brooklands, which is why the 'bullnose' in the picture has the compulsory 'Brooklands Can' silencer. With him is the great Harry Weslake whose scientific gas-flow tuning methods were developed on Sunbeams and were to oust the 'select the best engine and tune it' ways of George Dance. The photograph was taken at Brooklands after Cobbold had collected eleven world distance records for machines of 500–1000 cc.

Miss Olive M. Jones of Withington wrote to John Marston Ltd., on August 18th, 1928, enclosing this photograph.

'I feel I must write and tell you what a beautiful machine the Sunbeam is. I have driven all kinds of machines and find none of them to equal the Sunbeam, especially for comfort, reliability and speed.'

Francesco Franconi, awaits the off at the Sacconnex Hill Climb in September 1928. He made fastest time of the day and set a new climb record for both cars and motor cycles.

Franconi at rest in a nicely posed photograph with what looks like a pretty new Bullnose '90'. The continental racing men used to amaze the factory staff by ordering two and three racers at a time, and paying for them, then a contrast to the hard-up English. Today's fashion for putting 'Sunbeam' instead of a front number plate is not new.

The Swiss importer of Sunbeams was Edgard d'Eternod, whose agency was at 57, Pont d'Arve, Geneva. He was also a good rider, winner of the 500 cc sidecar class of the Grand Prix d'Europe. He is seen here with the outfit and Monsieur F. Francisquet.

Herr Mosslacher was another determined rider as this shot captioned 1928 GP d'Europe shows. European races were often held on comparatively short and flat tracks, a setting more or less unknown in England.

(Photo: The Bowers Collection)

Not surprisingly, after that forceful ride, Mosslacher won. Here he is being congratulated by Joseph Kollman, one-time Austrian Finance Minister, but now the Mayor of Baden. A Sunbeam win in Mitteleurope.

(Photo: Marston Palmer)

Above: The winning Sunbeam team for the Ilkley Grand National Trial of 1929, Eddie Flintoff, Charlie Helm and Vic Brittain. The team machines display a rugged individuality in style and preparation.

Left: A charming cyclist on a late 'twenties two-speed Ladies 'Golden' Sunbeam, in the all-black finish with 'Roman' alloy rims. Price new, 18 guineas (£18.18s.0d)

Right: The cycle is the 'RR' model 'Sporting Sunbeam' in all-black finish with Resilion Cantilever brakes and celluloid guards. Designed for the expert and wealthy rider who wished to cut a dash, it was the first Sunbeam without a Little Oil Bath since 1915.   *(Photo: Marston Palmer)*

Bauerheimber V. T. T. 1928 weg 20

Right: Birmingham's Jack Middleton on the stripped Sunbeam Road Racer which he rode in the 1928 Olympics in Amsterdam.

He was placed third in the British Solo Team Trial in 5 hrs. 24 m on a circuit of 103 miles. The team won the Silver Medal.

(Photo: Jack Middleton)

Left: L. Balazs on his way to winning the Hungarian Senior TT race of 1928 in a new record time. He also won in 1929.

A 'works' outfit with a difference. The 'box' or commercial sidecar has now virtually died out but was once a common sight. Though not catalogued, this coachbuilt outfit forms the subject of a publicity photograph. This photo was taken, as were most of the works photographs from 1915-1937, by Bennett Clark of Darlington Street, Wolverhampton, a superb photographer. *(Photo: Marston Palmer)*

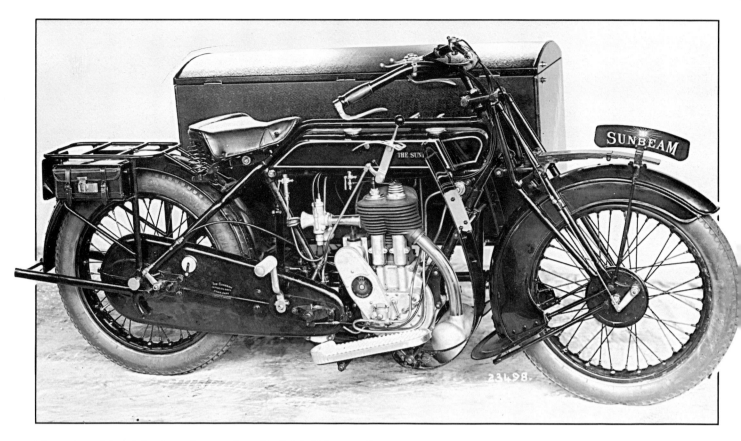

The other side of the box shows a late Model 7 600 cc, with mattress saddle and wired tyres (Dunlop Cord 26 x 3.50). The legshields were a common 'extra' on this model, though rarely seen today. It was also the last Sunbeam with footboards.

(Photo: Marston Palmer)

It's a nice period shot, even if the photographer focussed his camera to record the 1929 3.3 litre Roosevelt and caravan rather than the Sunbeam cyclists.

(Photo: Marston Palmer)

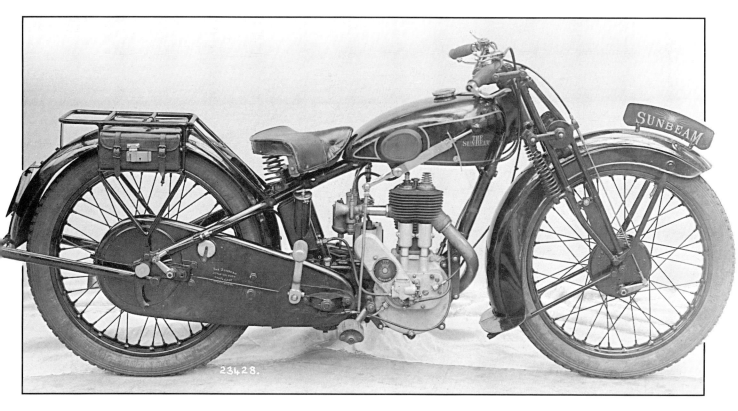

The rarity of the 'Bullnose' Sunbeams is explained by Sunbeam's having missed the 1928 change to the new saddle tank by the industry in common with their neighbours AJS. A hasty re-vamp was called for and from about September 1928 the new look was into production. Here is the prototype Model 1 347 cc originally registered UK5493, Engine No. 3001; Models 1 and 2 had a different frame, tanks and lubrication system from the rest of the range.

This is one of the works Junior TT racers for 1929. The photograph shows clearly the foot-change gearbox, extra fork dampers and 21 in front wheel. All three entries finished, highest place being Dodson's 4th, the previous year's lubrication problems having been overcome. The open pipes have mutes fitted.

TT practice with Dodson on UK 6449 wearing No. 1. and Australian A.E. 'Digger' Simcock No. 2. Behind Dodson is Percy Bischoff, who had been the curate of motorcycling writer 'Ixion' (Canon B.H. Davies) but had left the cloth and become Competition Manager at Marstons. Behind Simcock is the faithful Bert Tetstall. The front view shows the greater width of the racer's fuel tanks, which, however, looked standard from the side, in line with Sunbeam's policy of racing only modified production machines.

(Photo: The Bowers Collection)

Alec Bennett, by then an elder statesman amongst racing men and respected for his ability to win by thought rather than dash, signs on with the usual beautifully-prepared Sunbeam on 13th June 1929 for the 'Senior'. He was placed second at 70.05 mph.

Francesco Franconi signs on for the 1929 Senior. This fine rider had a bad year, retiring in the Junior race and running out of petrol in the Senior on his last rides for Sunbeam. His final TT appearance resulted in a 1932 11th place on a Velocette.

Dodson flat out in the 1929 TT.

A little of the shine has been taken off machine and rider but otherwise they are in fine shape at the finish. Behind, the press tend their camera gear.

(Photo: Marston Palmer)

Arthur Simcock taking Ramsey Hairpin in the 1929 Senior. He finished 7th despite a failing clutch. He was to be the TT'S first 'travelling marshal' in 1935 in a system where experienced ex-competitors were given fast machines and circulated the 37 mile course in case of trouble.

The TT fitters at Sunbeam c.1929. Centre front is Albert Collins, behind him Bert Tetstall.   *(Photo: The Dance Collection)*

SUNBEAMS AGAIN WIN THE SENIOR T.T. TEAM PRIZE

1929
1928
1927
1914

THE THIRD TIME IN SUCCESSION
AND THE FOURTH TIME IN ALL

THE 1929 WINNERS
MESSRS. A. SIMCOCK, C.J.P. DODSON
AND ALEC BENNETT.
ALL RIDING MODEL 90 SUNBEAMS

THE
TEAM
PRIZE

NOW WON
OUTRIGHT BY
SUNBEAMS

By Courtesy of "MOTOR CYCLING"

Makers:— John Marston Ltd., Sunbeamland, Wolverhampton.

Left: Under the eye of a 1929 camera, Albert Collins, Charlie Dodson, the then Mrs. Dodson and John Greenwood ponder the 1929 TT. The George Dance kneegrips turned on end and the high footrests point to Charlie's diminutive stature. Like Varzi, he went on to race cars.

Alec Bennett's, Charlie Dodson's and Arthur Simcock's signatures on three Sunbeam postcards.

(Photos: Marston Palmer)

THE SENIOR TOURIST TROPHY RACE
WON ON A SUNBEAM FOR THE
SECOND YEAR IN SUCCESSION AND THE FOURTH TIME IN ALL
1920 - 1922 - 1928 - 1929

THE WINNING 'BEAM!

Mr. C.J.P. DODSON
WINNER OF THE
SENIOR T.T. RACE
1928 - 1929

ALSO RECORD LAP
IN 30 MIN.47SEC.
= 73.55 M.P.H.

THE TROPHY

By Courtesy of
"MOTOR CYCLING"

Makers:- John Marston Ltd., Sunbeamland, Wolverhampton.

SUNBEAMS AGAIN WIN THE SENIOR T.T. TEAM PRIZE
1929
1928
1927
1914

THE THIRD TIME IN SUCCESSION
AND THE FOURTH TIME IN ALL

THE 1929 WINNERS
MESSRS. A.SIMCOCK, C.J.P. DODSON
AND ALEC BENNETT.
ALL RIDING MODEL 90 SUNBEAMS

THE
TEAM
PRIZE

NOW WON
OUTRIGHT BY
SUNBEAMS

By Courtesy of
"MOTOR CYCLING"

Makers:- John Marston Ltd., Sunbeamland, Wolverhampton.

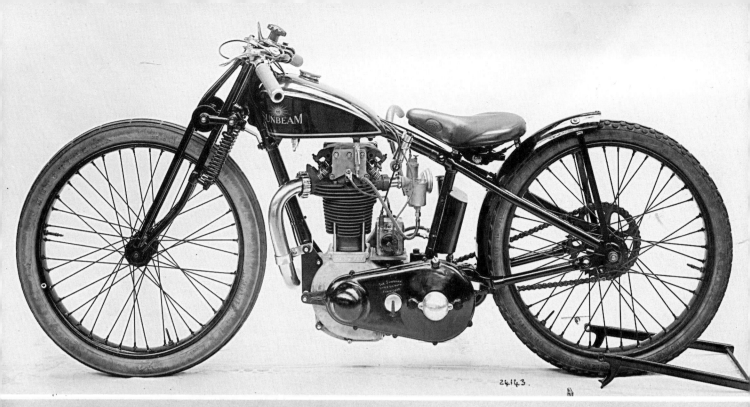

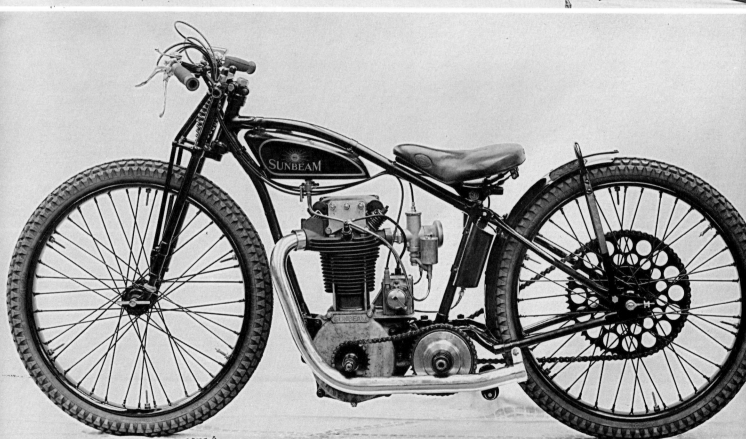

In 1929 Sunbeam joined in the enthusiasm for the new sport of Speedway by listing the Druid-forked machine at 85 guineas. It wasn't much use and was replaced by the Webb-forked and small-tanked variant. Only a few were made, though the single-port version of the '90' engine produced tremendous power and perhaps set the trend for the early 'thirties racers.

Opposite page: The great Achille Varzi in a natty 'twenties fashion ensemble on the Sunbeam with which he won the GP des Nations at Monza with a record lap at 94 mph. The bike sports a bulb-horn, no doubt for riding to and from the circuit.

Wearing the same sweater but with a change to checked trousers, Varzi holds the petrol hose with one hand whilst pouring in the oil with the other. Now we know why Model 90s had a left-hand oil filler! *(Photo: Marston Palmer)*

Opposite page top: Walsall's Vic Brittain, a recent recruit to the Sunbeam camp, after his win at the Lancashire Grand National in 1929. The helmet is the once-common high-crown style which gave way to the low-crown 'pudding-basin' beloved of today's traditional riders.

Opposite page bottom: Monsieur F. Francisquet in top gear on a European hillclimb, believed to be Argenteuil, or Donzelle, in 1929.

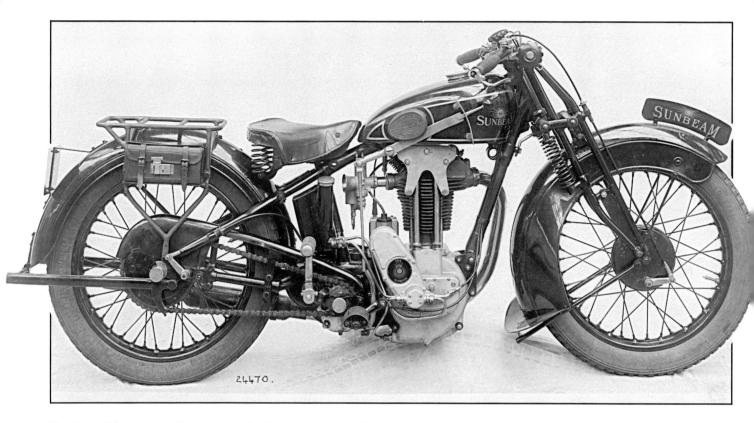

Reckoned by many riders to be the best-mannered Sunbeam of all was the single-port overhead valve in Model 8 350 cc, or Model 9 500 cc form shown here. In this prototype shot, the new-style rear carrier, with its detachable top, is unpainted. As in all factory shots of hand-change models, the gear lever is in a 'false neutral' to avoid obscuring 'The Sunbeam'.

Dated 26th November, 1929, this is the road-rider's racer. The Model 90 for 1930 is fitted with hand-change, silencers and standard fillers on petrol and oil tanks, the latter on the offside. The front wheel is, like the rear, of 19 in diameter. Many perfectly good Model 9s have been cut down to make bogus 'Model 90s' and it is worth checking for an 'NN' engine number and 'E' frame prefix before buying.

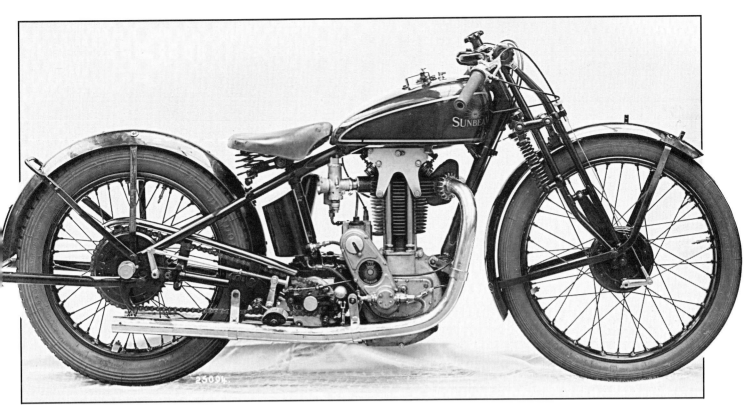

This is the racer's racer, which is fitted with the larger front-wheel, the rather odd foot-change and the oil filler on the 'pits' side. To many this is the most desirable saddle-tank Sunbeam with the rare uncluttered beauty of line not often found on road machines. In the 1930 TT it was hampered by the three-speed gearbox and the best placings were Dodson in 4th place, Tommy Bullus in 5th and Vic Brittain 8th. This was to be the end of serious racing at ICI Metals' John Marston Division.

The engine room of Sunbeam's 1930 racer. The armoured oil and petrol pipes were standard as was the high degree of finish and absence of polish on the aluminium. The clutch is adjusted by hand-wheel, as is the rear brake. The carburettor body, as with all vintage Sunbeams, is stamped with the model number 'M90'.

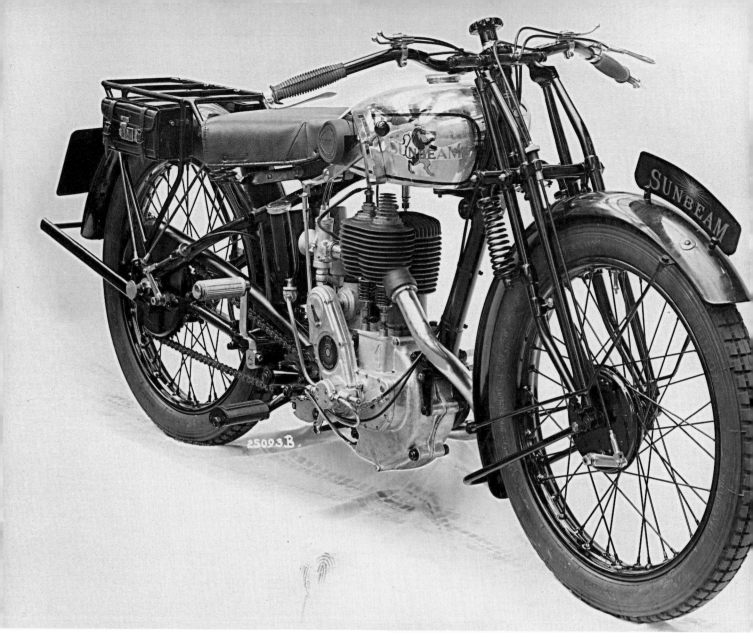

A model which didn't make the catalogues was the re-styled Model 6 with the 1930 Druid forks and the 1931 welded and chromed tank. It was also the first machine to bear the ICI group trademark, the Lion.

Harold Webb was a sporting motorcyclist of the old school, always owning fast Sunbeam outfits and riding long after he might have bought a car. Newly delivered is his 1930 Model 9 and No.9 sidecar.

(Photo: Roger Webb)

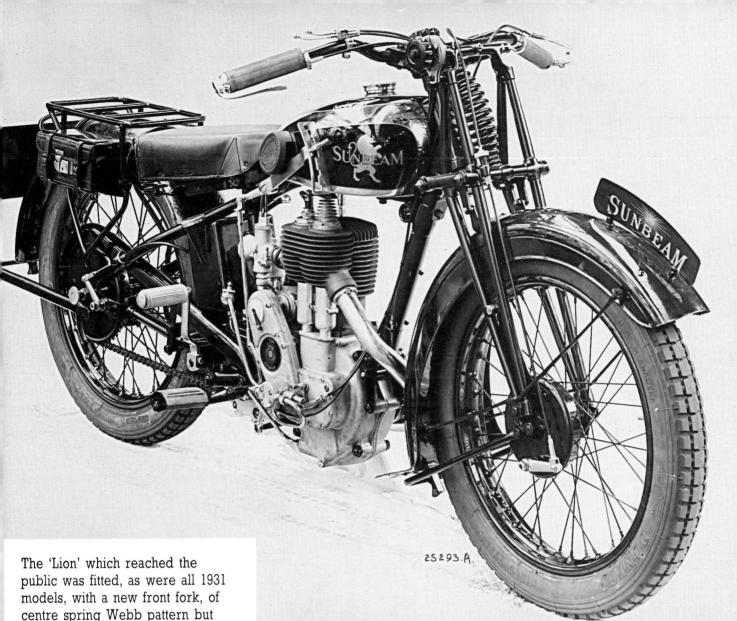

The 'Lion' which reached the public was fitted, as were all 1931 models, with a new front fork, of centre spring Webb pattern but made at Paul Street. Side-valve models still had the lever throttle, the then new 'twistgrip' reserved for the overhead valve Sunbeams. The front brake is still operated by the left hand, in traditional Sunbeam style like the cycles (though most machines have now been altered to the more universal right hand).

ICI Middle Eastern staff rode to Wolverhampton in 1931 on their Model 9s. They are photographed in front of the Elms works in the Penn Road which housed the competition department.

The main works is on the rise behind the car in the background. The Elms works is now a motor garage. *(Photo: Marston Palmer)*

The riders in the previous photograph are seen here at the Palestine border, a scene which has changed considerably in more recent years.

(Photo: Marston Palmer)

During 1930, the design was completed of a new Sunbeam engine, the 344 cc Model 10 of 74 mm x 80 mm. Here is the first completed engine, hand-filing marks visible. The projection on the rocker-box is for the hand gear-change lever, bolted directly to the engine.

(Photo: Marston Palmer)

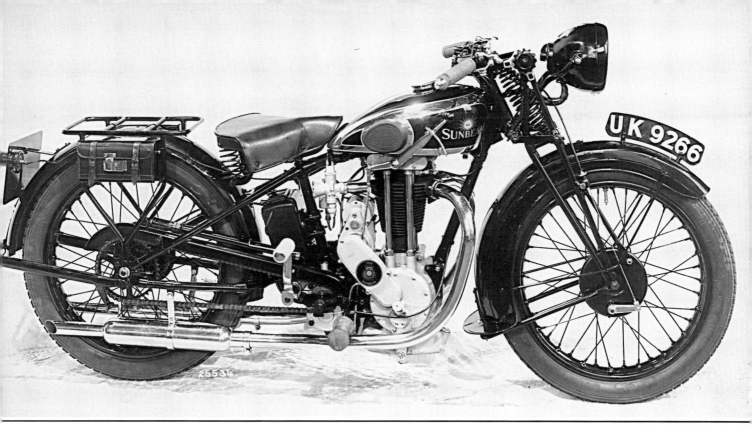

The Model 10 road-tested by *The Motor Cycle* was one of the prototypes, UK9266, now in Australia, but shown here, as manufactured, in a Bennett Clark photograph. The anonymous tester said 'It is perfectly straightforward in design, is fast, smooth, comfortable and handles superbly at both high and low speeds'. It was only £60, cheap for a Sunbeam, but failed to find many buyers.

Sunbeams, like most makers, had never actually made their own-branded sidecars. For 1931 they offered a new No. 14 sidecar shown here with a Model 9. It cost £21, complete.

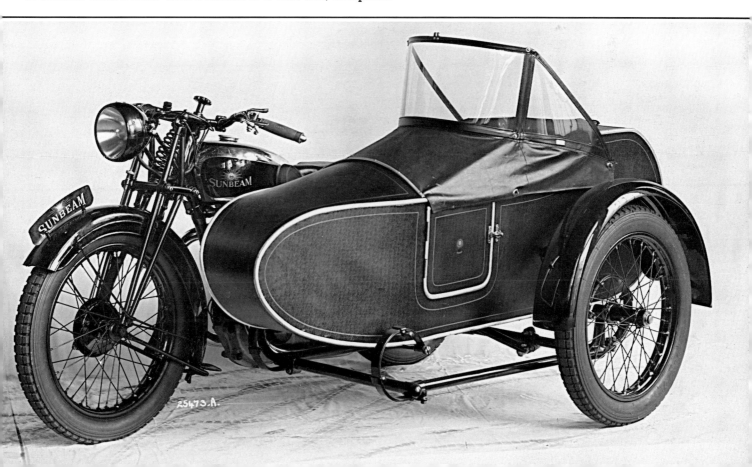

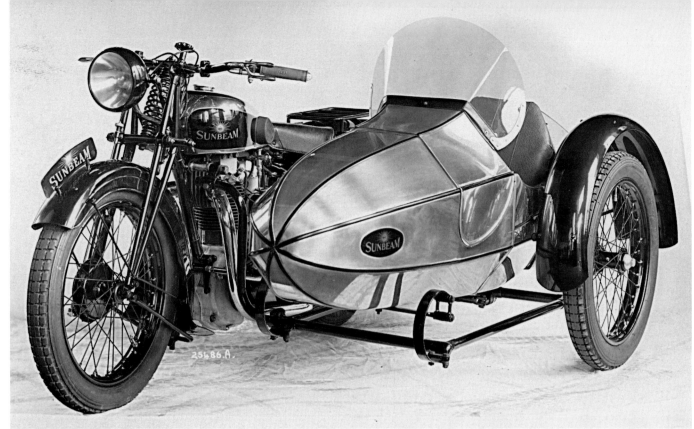

Opposite page top: Rather more sporting was the No. 9 sidecar in polished aluminium at £20.

Opposite page bottom: For 1931 the 90 was catalogued as either a 'road racing' machine or as a 'fast touring' bike with hand change and normal footrests. A full rear oilbath could be fitted for an extra £2.10.0., a tacit admission that the design's racing days were perhaps coming to an end.

Ever - cheerful Joe Sarkis faces the camera with his mechanic, Tom Mackie, after winning the South African Senior TT in January 1932. The machine is a 1931 Model 90. *(Photo: Marston Palmer)* 83

Here is Frank Williams in racing gear aboard a works hybrid Sunbeam 90 with 1931-style engine and 1933 foot-change for the 1932 Manx Grand Prix in which he finished 8th. Journalist J. S. Ward is on his left.

(Photo: Ray Jones)

The 1933 machines were virtually as for 1932 but with the addition of tank-mounted instruments on the larger models. Back from the dead was the 1933 350 Model 8, almost unchanged from its last listing in 1930 even to its three-speed gears.

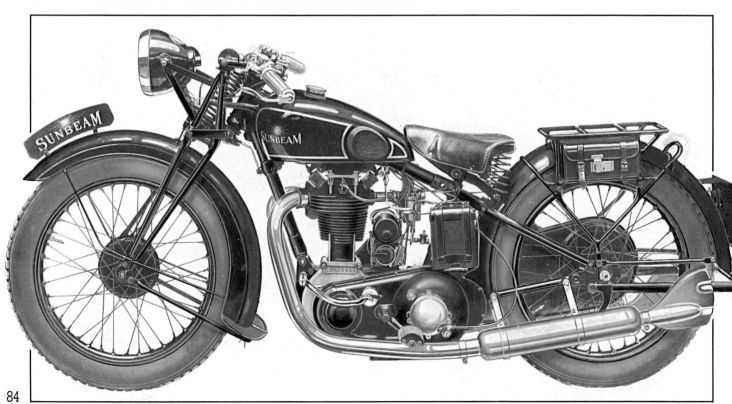

The photographer's stamp on this photograph says 1.9.32, the Model 9 for the 1933 catalogue. It also bears the handwritten comment 'Use same block 1934 as 1933' which sums up the changes to the model in that period.

Sunbeams were now trying to compete at the, to them, 'lower end' of the market, and tried a 250 'Longstroke' of 70 mm bore and 90 mm stroke, though, unlike the other famous 'Longstroke', it was overhead valve. Not many buyers were found for 250s, but the factory succeeded in cashing in on two famous names at once by producing a variant called the 'Little 90', a racer with foot change gears and appropriate styling.

Photographed in 1932, the faithful 500 cc Lion for 1933. A handsome bike, if tending a little to middle age and overweight.

Although the name of W. Heath Robinson cannot be found on the factory roll for 1933, his influence is apparent in the splendid 'Electric Robot Cycle Testing Machine'. Lineshafting wheels, bored off centre, bicycle chainwheels and a 1932 motorcycle chaincase, complete with 'Little Oil Bath' transfer, combine to drive the machine by its pedals over a very undulating 'road' whilst carrying 150 lbs.

One of the cycles tested would have been this Tourist Silver Sunbeam, one of the increasing number of cheaper bicycles being made without the Little Oil Bath. 'One of Marston's troubles is that they make too good a product' said a factory memo.

Frank Williams, one of the Sunbeam Trials Team for 1934. As the company dropped out of the road-racing sphere, it concentrated its efforts on reliability trials, gaining some solid successes. The two prongs on the front fork are for the rider's number plate.   *(Photo: Marston Palmer)*

Second member of the team was Norman Hooton. Post World War 2, he was at the James factory and formed, with Norman Palmer and Norman Moore, the famous 'Three Normans' trials team on James 125 ML models.

Opposite page top: The sidecar muscle was provided by N.P.O. Bradley and the everlasting Bert Tetstall as sidecar passenger with Bradley's well set-up 600 cc Model 9 outfit. Peter Bradley was an outstanding sidecar driver, winning many events and having a great ability to get to the finish under the most adverse conditions.

Opposite page bottom: But alas, trials bikes do not stay clean! Here are the members of the trials team again in the interval between competing in an unknown trial and getting out the brush and hosepipe. The white coats were official company wear but for photographs only, not for the dirty work.

Opposite page: 26th May, 1933, says the stamp on the back of this photograph of the new Model 95R. This is the prototype using a single-port Model 9 crankcase. The finish speaks for itself. *(Photo: Marston Palmer)*

The prototype again. The large tank now envelops the front of the saddle and the machine has the rocking-pedal footchange with its mechanism inside the metal case behind the crankcase. A very handsome motor cycle, the company's last from the hand of John Greenwood who was to retire in April 1934. Its most notable rider was Walter Rusk. *(Photo: Marston Palmer)*

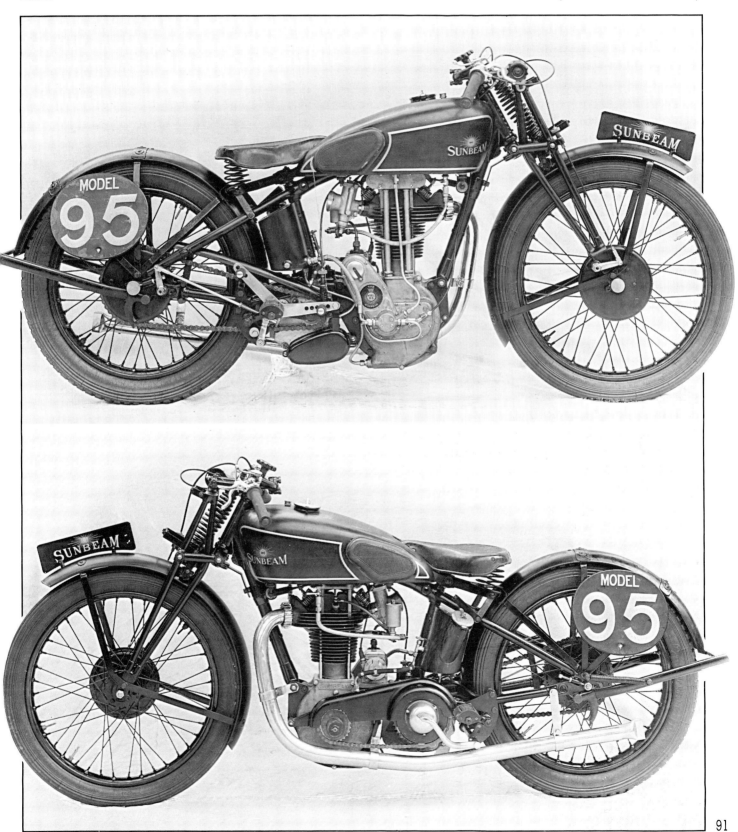

The 1933 'Little 90' was re-styled for 1934 to become the 'Little 95' with a four-gallon tank and 8.4:1 compression.

Without even a Sunbeam transfer, the Model 9 sidecar cost £17-8-6 complete. It was made by Swallow in Blackpool.

One which didn't reach production was this 500 cc Lion with the footchange and clutch operation of a Model 95. The matt alloy and superb enamel is well in evidence even on an experimental or special order bike like this.

The only big news for 1935 was the George Stephenson-designed 250. It was the first Sunbeam to have a bought-in gearbox and its engine sported hairpin springs and a deep timing case. The bulbous silencer made a pleasant noise but little success came its way.

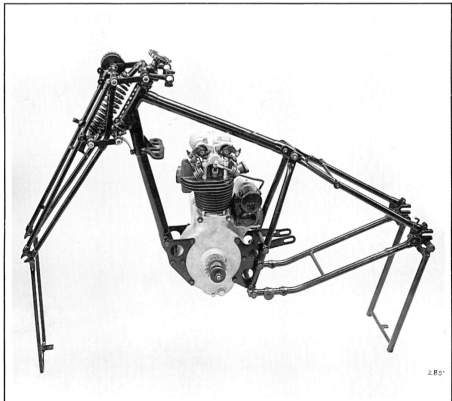

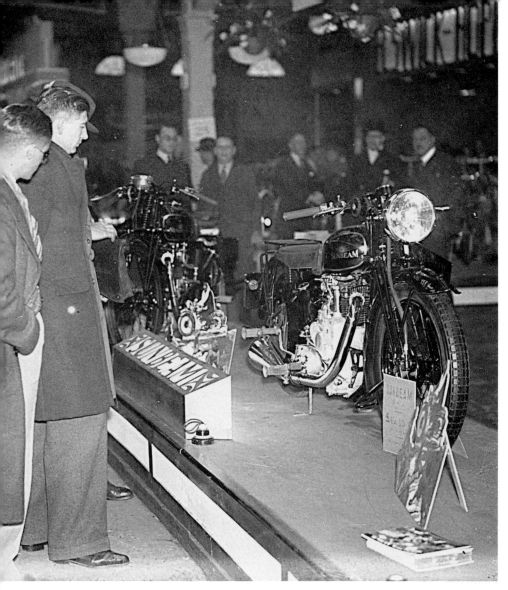

The Sunbeam stand at the 1934 Olympia Show with the new 250 on display.

The 250 complete. It has been said that a handsome motor cycle has its frame so full that it is impossible to spit through! The 250 followed that dictum but, nevertheless, lasted for one season only. It cost but £49 - 10s - 0d, plus £5 - 10s - 0d for the electric lighting set.

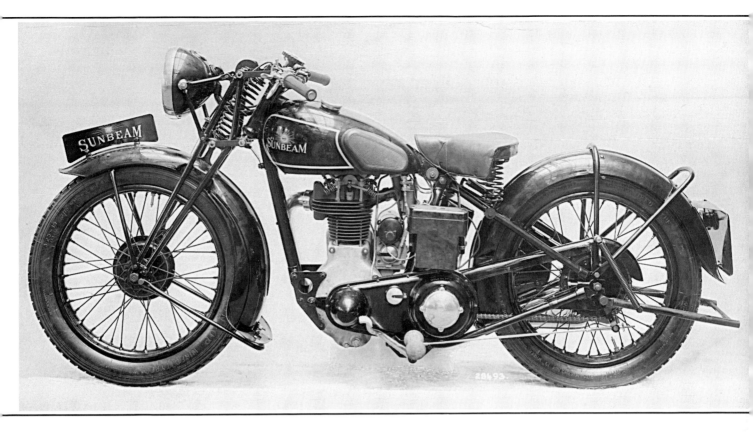

Somehow the near-side of a British motor cycle never looks as good as the off-side and Sunbeam's new model was no exception. Most of the trouble is caused by the 'bolt-on' battery and lights, few makers enclosing them until after World War 2.

For 1935 the Model 95 appeared in two guises. The racer, to an improved version of the 1934 specification, was the 95R, whilst a fast road version was the 95L (for lighting). 'Speed approximately 85 mph on 50/50 petrol benzol' was the factory's note on the back of this photograph. (Both engine and frame were stamped 95L or 95R so look for this if buying a 'genuine racer').

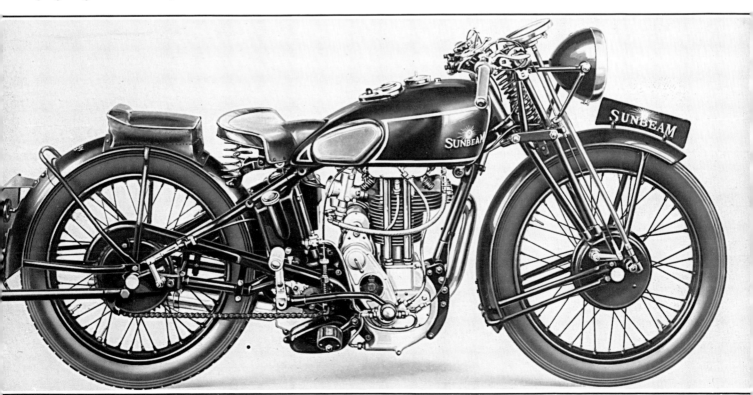

Mrs. Angelina Webb, wife of Harold, at Pendine Sands on the family Model 95L and launch sidecar in the 1930s. Photographs of Sunbeam's faster models going on ordinary journeys loaded with the family's camping gear are, understandably, pretty rare.

(Photo: Roger Webb)

Again, from the top. By 1935 the front brake had gone to the – normal – right-hand lever and the throttle had an Amal (also made by ICI) straight-pull twistgrip. The old air lever is now used only for starting while the left-hand one is still for the manual ignition control. The clutch is second from the left, the valve lifter, for easy starting, far left. The right-hand pedal is the gear-change, the left the rear brake.

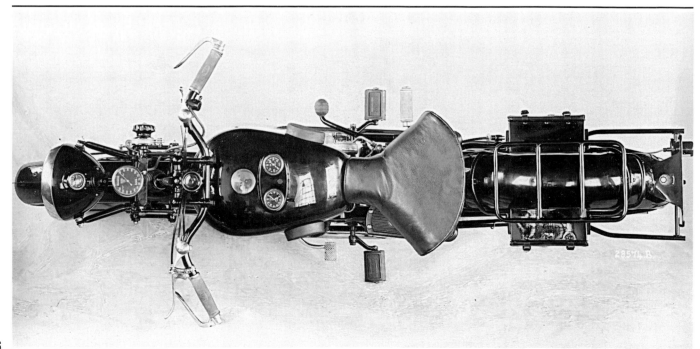

Some re-design had been done in time for the 1936 season, on the engine where the ohv models had lost the prominent front finning as the result of a more central and larger exhaust. The 'dog-leg' front fork and its interchangeable wheel had also gone. A new and simplified numbering system for cycles and motorcycles was introduced in 1936.

The big change for 1936, much to the dismay of some people who worked on the production line, was the dropping of Sunbeam's own gearbox in favour of a proprietary Burman. This meant that the rear chain drive moved to the nearside of the bike, rather than the offside as in bicycle practice. The frame also had a duplex loop under the engine.

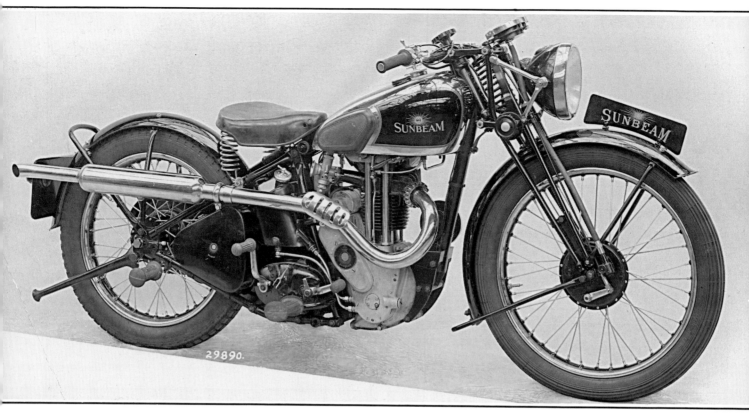

For the last season at Wolverhampton, Sunbeams finally managed to clean up the engine, making the oil pump and its connections internal. The rocker feed remains rather visible now on this 350 cc Sports, Series 2. The lining of the chrome tank panels was blue as well as gold. Price £66. 20 brake horsepower at 6000 rpm gave a top speed of 75 mph, according to Sunbeam figures.

As in the 1936 range, the 1937 Model 9, Series 2, and its 600 cc brother had Sunbeam's interesting decompressor where the cable worked a ramp system inside the exhaust cam wheel to lift the exhaust cam follower. It was ingenious but leaked oil through the gland and wore rapidly. Its cable is just behind the exhaust pipe. The Model 9 cost £75, gave 25 bhp at 6000 rpm and did 75 mph.

Purchased new in Melbourne for £A137, this 1937 Model 9 Series 2 was photographed in 1939. The Sunbeam is now owned by Lawrence Moloney, son of the original owner. The Australia-made Dusting sidecar was a further £A38 in 1938.

(Photo: Lawrence Moloney)

The weight and electrical complexity which had been added to the Longstroke engine since 1922 are clearly shown here. The reflection in the tank is the glass clerestory roof of the Elms works. This pattern of tank knee grip is also found on AMC and post-war BSA Sunbeams.

The last Marston engine project was this 500 cc side-valve motor designed by Dougal Marchant. It was to have been of unit-construction with fully enclosed rear chain. Primary drive was by gear and the alloy head had a squish-band combustion chamber. It was road tested as JML 226 but was removed by Marchant at the AMC takeover in September 1937.

GENERAL SPECIFICATION

FRAME . . .	Duplex cradle type with three-point rubber-insulated petrol tank mounting.
STANDS . . .	Fitted to front and rear wheels. Rear stand spring-up type. Prop stand.
HANDLEBARS .	Sunbeam adjustable with steering damper. Combined lever mountings.
FORKS . . .	Central spring pattern designed to give first class road-holding qualities. Fitted with shock absorber.
WHEELS . . .	Detachable rear wheel. For Models 9 and Lion Side Valve the wheels are quickly detachable and interchangeable. Sports Models wheel rims are chromium-plated with black centres edged in blue.
TRANSMISSION	Front chain totally enclosed in Sunbeam patent oil bath chaincase. Rear chain adequately protected with automatic lubrication controlled by regulator. Sunbeam shock absorber on engine shaft.
BRAKES . . .	Internal expanding front and rear. 250 c.c., 350 c.c. and Light Solo Models, 6 in. diameter, other models, 8 in. diameter.
SILENCER . .	Special type ensuring quiet exhaust note without loss of engine efficiency.
ENGINE LUBRICATION .	Dry sump system with internal oil pumps and leads. Oil tank fitted on seat tube.
CARBURETTER	Amal needle jet pattern. Twist grip control.
PETROL TANK	Models 9 and Lion: Capacity approximately 3 gallons. Other models approximately 2¼ gallons. On the Sports Models the tank is chrome-plated with black panels lined blue and gold.
TOOLS	Comprehensive kit enclosed in all-metal toolbox. Tyre inflator.

EXTRAS (if ordered with new machine)

	£	s.	d.
Speedometer fitted on top of fork girder with enclosed drive inside front brake drum	2	10	0
Ditto with 5 in. dial	5	5	0
Carrier easily detachable (Models 250 c.c., 350 c.c. and Light Solo)		12	6
Carrier easily detachable (Models 9 and Lion)		17	6
Pillion seat		12	6
Pillion footrests (folding pattern)		12	6
Legshields	1	15	0
Rear chaincase (Models 250 c.c. and 350 c.c.)		2	0
Rear chaincase (all other models)		2	5

SPECIAL NOTE: All machines will be fitted with speedometer unless otherwise specified

For details of Sidecars and Terms of Guarantee see Full Catalogue

Made by Sunbeam Motor Cycles, London, S.E.18

Telephone No.: Woolwich 1010

SUNBEAM MOTOR CYCLES 1938

LION SIDE VALVE MODEL (SERIES 2)

SIDE VALVE MODELS

500 c.c. LION LONGSTROKE (Series 2)   Ref. No. A.29

ENGINE . . . Sunbeam single cylinder. Alloy head. Totally enclosed lubricated valves. Special alloy piston. Bore 77 mm., stroke 105·5 mm., capacity 492 c.c.
GEARBOX . . Silent constant mesh; four speed; footchange.
GEAR RATIOS Solo: 5·0 to 1; 6·3 to 1; 7·85 to 1; 13·3 to 1. Sidecar: 5·26 to 1; 6·64 to 1; 8·26 to 1; 14·1 to 1.
Lucas magdyno lighting with voltage control.   Electric horn.

PRICE 68 Guineas NET CASH (Including electric lighting and horn)

600 c.c. LION LONGSTROKE (Series 2)   Ref. No. A.30

ENGINE . . . Specification as 500 c.c. Model. Bore 85 mm., stroke 105·5 mm., capacity 598 c.c.
GEARBOX . . Silent constant mesh; four speed; footchange.
GEAR RATIOS Solo: 5·0 to 1; 6·3 to 1; 7·85 to 1; 13·3 to 1. Sidecar: 5·26 to 1; 6·64 to 1; 8·26 to 1; 14·1 to 1.
Lucas magdyno lighting with voltage control.   Electric horn.

PRICE 70 Guineas NET CASH (Including electric lighting and horn)

A fully illustrated Catalogue can be obtained from your local dealer or will be sent post free on receipt of a postcard addressed to Sunbeam Motor Cycles, London, S.E.18.

Telephone No.: Woolwich 1010

'Sunbeam Motor Cycles, London, S.E. 18' said the transfer, but otherwise the range was unchanged for 1938 under the new management. The frame and engine numbers had an 'A' prefix added to the Marston numbers by AMC, as the Wolverhampton parts were used up in London. Meanwhile, the decision was taken to continue the Sunbeam name with a new range. The catalogues for cycle and motorcycle had a script 'Sunbeam' logo in red on a yellow ground, and the sharp practice of charging customers an extra fee for the now compulsory speedometer had begun.

Another way of getting two people on to a Sunbeam, was to buy a tandem. AMC had bought the Sunbeam trademark to add to their cycle range and kept the old Marston models and model numbers. It is probable that many Sunbeam tandems and sporting cycles have not been identified as such because of painted-over transfers and the absence of the distinctive 'Little Oil Bath'.

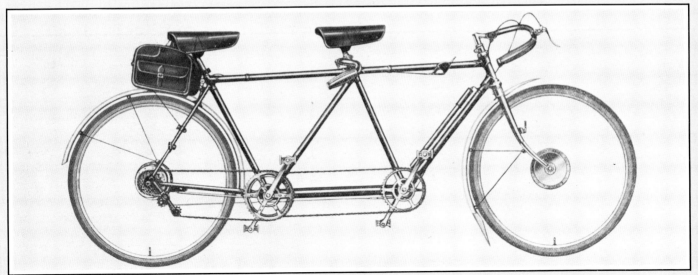

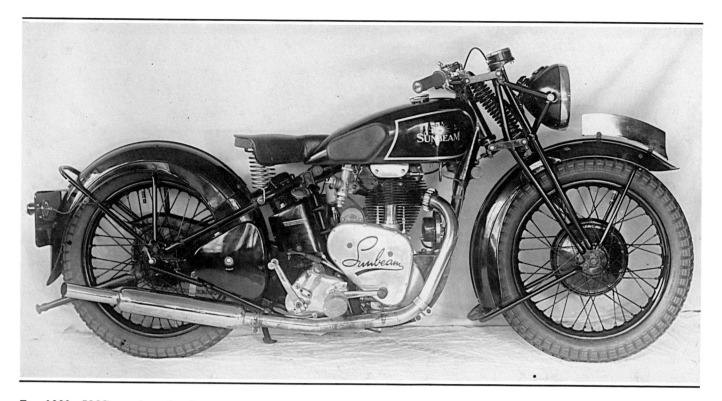

For 1939, AMC produced a line-up of entirely new Sunbeams, formed by re-badging an AJS. The engines were totally new, with the 'Sunbeam' script from the 1939 catalogue cover cast into the huge timing case. The engineering was very competently carried out, with full pressure lubrication and some filtration of the oil. Described, and known since, as the Sunbeam 'Hi-cam' they were good bikes but were made for a short time only, the design a casualty of World War 2. This is the 350 cc B24.

The new range for 1939 used the same base with three different styles. This is the 347 cc B24S 'Sports' in prototype form with unpainted mudguards and unchromed silencer. In production the tank would be chromed with black panels lined in blue and gold. High compression piston, polished head and the check-spring front forks shown completed this now rare motorcycle.

Rarest of all is the competition model B24T with cutaway tank, Dunlop saddle and polished engine internals. The ISDT variant used in the 1939 trial by Geoff Godber-Ford weighed 428 lbs all up, though, and not many of the standard version were sold.

The unchanging Longstroke models were carried on by AMC still with ICI's Lion name. They remained unchanged until the end of AMC production. (The reason that these AMC photographs were so poor compared to those of Bennett Clark was that at AMC the photograph was only used as the basis for re-touching, every part being brushed over before use in the catalogue.)

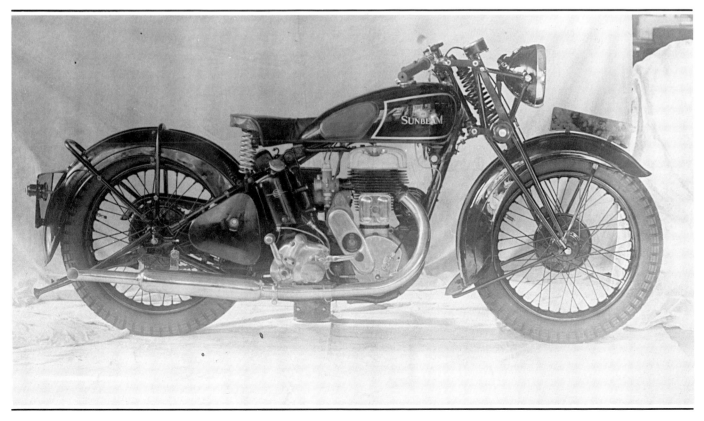

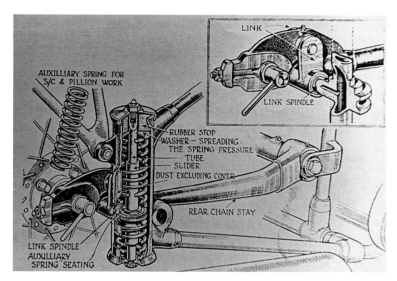

The new innovation was to be rear springing by a combination of swinging arm and plungers. Some were made, at least one being photographed post-war in Australia.

For 1940, the range was as before. Here are two of the AMC photographs for the catalogue, dated 24 January 1940, so heavily re-touched as to be virtually paintings. The offside view is of the 500 cc C23 single, the nearside of the 500 cc C25.

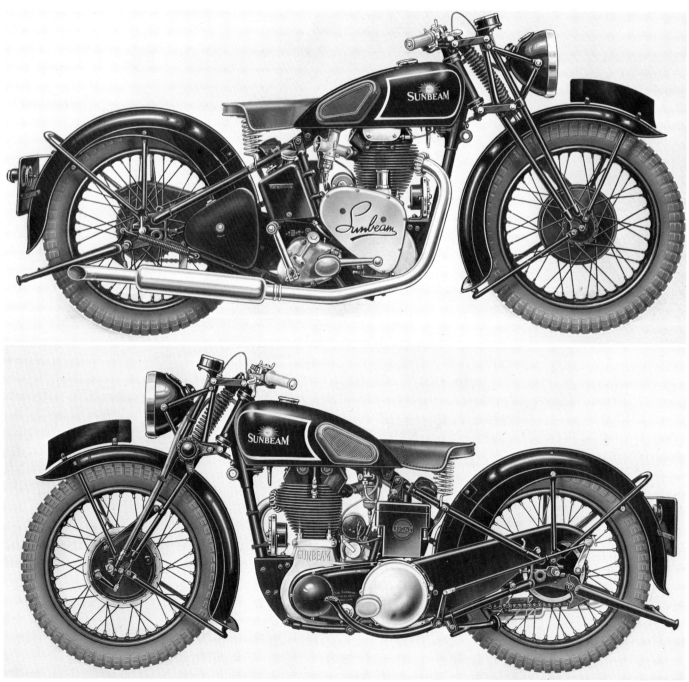

The Plumstead factory also made a prototype 1000 cc AMC-engined V-twin for the military sidecar-wheel-drive market. Fitted with heavyweight Teledraulic forks, reverse gear and low-ratio gearbox it competed with the Norton 'Big 4'. Here are Sgt. Jack Williams, Sgt. J.W. 'Crasher' White and Sgt. Major Bob McGregor with the outfit. It was not produced and the sole prototype was broken up after the war.

(Photo: R.F. Currie)

BSA's post-war Sunbeam was Erling Poppe's re-design of the BMW R75 (as was their 125 cc Bantam a copy of the DKW R125). Instead of a flat-twin, an earlier BSA engine was adapted with a complex overhead-cam, cross-flow cylinder head. Here the former Sunbeam works rider George Dance is seen on the prototype which was capable of 90 mph. The engine did not reach production in this form but the rest of the machine with its BMW-style forks, suspension and 16 in tyres did.

BSA made a rigid-frame, BMW-style prototype which *Motor Cycling* thought would be marketed as 'an alternative to the springer'. It never was. Here it is with the S7, designer Erling Poppe sitting on it, shaking hands with Mike Nedham of BSA Redditch. The S7 was designed and made there, not at BSA Small Heath. As may be noticed, the engine has no flexible mounting but has identical tyres, front and rear. The wheels were detachable in two minutes without needing spanners and the intention was, presumably, to market a sidecar outfit with spare wheel. This never happened.

Opposite page top: GOC 219 again (with re-touched number plate). The carburettor cover and exhaust system are completely different from production versions as is the BMW-style rear-drive mounting. The engine's height was a problem when installed in the type of frame originally designed for a flat-twin. The 'Line Ahead Twin' designed in 1932, which inspired the S7's engine, had a front-mounted shaft-drive to the valve gear.

Opposite page middle: Here is FON 992 once more, converted to the new cylinder-head – which gave less power but cut down rear drive wear – as tested by *Motor Cycling* in 1946. The sycophantic test praised aspects of the S7 which did not exist, namely its great smoothness and precise handling. The early S7s with rigid engine mounting vibrated badly and good handling had to wait until the re-design during 1948. The finish, at least, was traditional Sunbeam black, though without gold leaf.

Opposite page bottom: The early series-production version of the S7. The engine is now rubber-mounted – the flexible connection in the exhaust is beneath the kick-starter – and the speedometer has reached its final position. In this form the S7 was reliable enough though the undamped front and rear springing was a poor design feature on a luxury motorcycle, as was the combined centre and prop stand which toppled the machine over if touched in the wrong place. Few survive because the motorcycling public bought few, despite the praise which the manufacturer-controlled motorcycle journals heaped upon the design. The poor sales were perhaps because of its clumsy appearance as much as the machine's reputation for unreliability. Tank badges had a blue background.

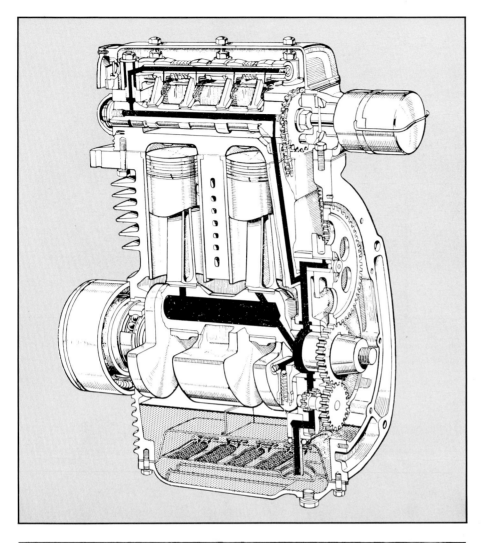

The general engine layout of the early S7 is shown in this cutaway drawing. The crankshaft and rods are suitable for a much higher power output than the cylinder head can provide but the tiny gear pump at the rear has a pre-war air about it as does the absence of any serious attempt at oil filtration.

Later engines were fitted with a larger capacity oil sump and an adjustable plunger cam-chain tensioner in place of the early Weller type. Problems with the unit in service were largely confined to the cylinder-head joint – which was difficult to make leakproof – and a high degree of valve-gear wear.

'Monty', otherwise Viscount Montgomery of Alamein, victor in the Desert War, is photographed taking delivery of the S7 presented to him at the 1948 Earl's Court Show. It would be difficult to think of a less appropriate gift for a short and light Field Marshal than a motorcycle weighing four hundredweight. There is no evidence that he ever rode it and it was sold off, after his death, to a motor museum.

Opposite page top: For the 1949 Season the S7 was offered in Mist-Green – a light pea-green – as well as black, though there is no reason to suppose that any original-style S7s were supplied in this colour. The photograph shows the central spring unit linking the two front-fork legs. The air-filter cover is the type fitted to later models. The price was £200 plus £54 Purchase Tax, with the speedometer charged as a non-optional extra at £4 plus £1 1s 8d Purchase Tax.

During 1949 the S7 metamorphosed into the S7 de luxe, with standard BSA suspension front and rear, giving effective damping at last. The clean handlebars were replaced with standard BSA controls and the only colour was Mist-Green. In this form, the S7 de luxe remained in the catalogue until 1956, selling in relatively small numbers. The price was £204 plus £55 1s 8d Purchase Tax. At least the speedometer, required by law, appeared to be no longer charged as an extra but BSA had simply put up the machine's price by its exact cost.

Tank badges had a yellow background.

The new variant for the 1949 season was the S8, a much lighter version of the S7 fitted with BSA twin-type suspension and 18 in and 19 in wheels and tyres. This sold quite well at first and, as many have said, it might well have been the model needed back in 1946. A well set-up one is a joy to ride though still lacking in top speed and acceleration despite the cast silencer's sporty design and the machine's lighter weight.

Having developed a four-cylinder engine for a projected, but cancelled, light car, BSA tried it out in a modified S7 with front-mounted radiators. It failed and was scrapped, the engine remaining intact.

The optional finish for the S8 was an attractive 'Polychromatic Gun-Metal Grey' which tones well with the cast-aluminium engine unit and silencer.

The final form of the 'Golden' Sunbeam was this 1952 'Light Tourist' produced until the 1957 takeover of the Sunbeam trademark by Raleigh. The essential features are still those of the pre-First War Sunbeam, the chaincase recognisably a Carter. Later versions had an extremely well-designed, quickly detachable rear wheel which left the chain and sprocket in the chaincase, a modification which Sunbeam riders of seventy years earlier would have enjoyed.

SUNBEAM Light Tourist
Model WR3

21in. and 23in. all-brazed frame; fork with D to round blades, with brazed-in ends, central in blades. 26in. x 1⅜in. Westwood rims. Dunlop Roadster tyres. B.S.A. 3-speed hub with B.S.A. 'Snap' control; Twist Grip control 3/8 extra. Sunbeam 'Little Oilbath' gearcase. Comfort bend handlebar. Spearpoint front guard with chromium tip. Prop stand. Terry 'Extracoil' saddle. Roller lever brakes with quick-release stirrups and finger adjustment to rear brake. Finish, black and chrome. Metal head badge. Alternative finish, green, 7/5 extra. B.S.A. Hublite with stand-by battery, £2 . 11 . 10 extra.

£19 . 5 . 5 (tax paid)

The Scintillating **BSA SUNBEAM**

The last appearance of the Sunbeam name on a powered two-wheeler was on this 1959 motor-scooter. Made in 175 cc two-stroke and 250 cc four-stroke variants, the BSA-Sunbeam scooter – which bore John Marston's elegant badge in gilt plastic – was a workmanlike machine. It arrived long after the Italian scooters were entrenched, though, and teething troubles with the first ones – a BSA tradition – didn't help sales. The Edward Turner-designed 250, in particular, would top 70 mph and handled well, but it faded out in 1964 along with its identical twin, the Triumph Tigress.